HEY KIDS!

Out the Door, Let's Explore!

D1411349

Other Redleaf Press books by Rhoda Redleaf

Learn and Play the Green Way (2009)

HEY KIDS! Out the Door, Let's Explore!

Rhoda Redleaf

Redleaf Press®
www.redleafpress.org
800-423-8309

Published by Redleaf Press
10 Yorkton Court
St. Paul, MN 55117
www.redleafpress.org

First edition 2010
Cover design by Jenny Larson
Cover photographs by Jenny Larson (background image, top left, and back cover) and Getty Images (bottom right)
Interior typeset in Futura and designed by Brad Norr Design
Printed in the United States of America
16 15 14 13 12 11 10 09   1 2 3 4 5 6 7 8

Library of Congress Cataloging-in-Publication Data
Redleaf, Rhoda.
  Hey kids! out the door, let's explore! / Rhoda Redleaf.
      p. cm.
  Includes bibliographical references.
  ISBN 978-1-933653-91-4
  1. Hiking. 2. Infants—Walking. 3. Parent and child. 4. Family recreation. 5. Nature study. I. Title.
  GV199.5.R44 2010
  796.51—dc22
                          2009006693

Printed on 30 percent post-consumer waste paper

Hey Kids! Out the Door, Let's Explore!

Concept Walks

Appendixes

Preface

Fifty-five years ago, I graduated from Sarah Lawrence College as a newly certified nursery school teacher and went to work in the college's summer preschool program. During the summer we took numerous and extensive trips with the children exploring our neighborhood, the natural environment surrounding our school, and the college campus. Our classrooms were always a hub of activities as the children re-created the places they visited in their block and dramatic play, in murals or dioramas, through storytelling and play acting, and by making exhibits of their collections with dictated commentaries. The words *emergent curriculum* were not known at that time, and it would be many years before the Reggio Emilia approach was adopted in the United States. The model we all tried to achieve was called the Human Relationships Laboratory (the subtitle of the early childhood education "bible" of the day, *The Nursery School* by Katherine Read). The emphasis was always on the child.

But times changed! The Russians launched Sputnik and over the next decades there was a growing pressure to teach academics to younger and younger children. Research in its own way contributed to this thrust as we learned that young children actually do learn what teachers teach but not always with true understanding. In the course of my professional career, I have seen the focus in early childhood education shift through every domain of child development. I have both studied and taught each developmental domain. As

I wrote curriculum books in the 1980s and early 1990s to meet the training needs of teacher-directed programming in preschool, I prefaced each collection of activities with introductory explanations of the philosophy of child-centered learning, which I always felt was crucial.

It is a real thrill for me to see that my basic approach to early childhood education has come into its own again in emergent curriculum. (It actually never completely left my training grounds at Sarah Lawrence and similar places.) I marvel at the way writer/editor Megan Davis so beautifully adapted my words from the original books to fit the emergent curriculum model. Of course an emphasis on language development has always been crucial to me and that focus remains central in each walk in this book. Be sure to read Megan's excellent introduction, which highlights features of the Reggio Emilia approach and the role of language in learning.

Times and technologies continue to change, and we are privileged to live in an age of such advanced technology, although that in itself can be overwhelming. Carefully used, technology can give us many rewards. Many Web sites exist that can support the focus of your walks with children. Your local librarian can help you find them. We use this technology to include related activities, songs, and verses from *Open the Door, Let's Explore More*, the inspiration for this book, as PDF files on the Redleaf Press Web site. You can download them at www.redleafpress.org.

Enter "Hey Kids!" into the search field and follow the links.

The most important learning task of young children remains constructing their own knowledge to make sense of their world. You, the adults in their world, provide the bridges from the unknown to the known. I hope this book helps you find the tremendous learning potential available in common everyday experiences.

Rhoda Redleaf
St. Paul, Minnesota

Acknowledgments

Looking back over a very long career of teaching and writing I see many people who played a crucial role in shaping that career. I am thankful for my teachers and mentors at Sarah Lawrence College who provided the foundation for my work, and those at Erikson Institute who nurtured it along in later years when I returned for graduate studies. Throughout my career I was inspired and additionally trained by my colleagues at the Minnesota Association for the Education of Young Children and the National Association for the Education of Young Children. I am especially grateful to my husband, Paul, who not only has encouraged and supported me through all these years, but additionally has always offered very tangible help (which, in this case, meant hours of dealing with technical computer problems with the remote assistance of our son, Eric, in Phoenix).

Several other people deserve special recognition for their important roles in bringing this book to fruition. I am exceedingly grateful for their help and wish to express sincere thanks to the following people:

Linda Hein, publisher at Redleaf Press, and David Heath, editor-in-chief, for their decision to publish this book. Megan Davis, for outstanding editorial work in shaping the content of this book to the most current and desirable program models. Kyra Ostendorf, acquisitions and development editor, for putting all of our work together in the most coherent, consistent, and readable form in an efficient and competent way while remaining a complete joy to work with. Laura Maki, along with her capable team, for shepherding this book through the production process.

The librarians and staff of the Children's Room of the St. Paul Public Library, who helped me find the numerous books listed with each walk—and whose workload was enormously increased by the hundreds and hundreds of books I left on carts on the many days I worked there.

I have been writing about field trips throughout my entire professional career. These writings have been in the form of training guides, curriculum guides, a film strip, teaching units, special bulletins, newsletters, and the first book I wrote, *Open the Door, Let's Explore*—the grandfather of this publication. I want to thank all of the people who guided me through all those productions in my various work settings:

- the staff at Resources for Child Caring and earlier Toys 'N Things Press
- the University of Minnesota Center for Early Education and Development (CEED) program
- the Minnesota Department of Human Services
- the St. Paul Public Schools

I am indebted to a huge percentage of the early childhood education community in Minnesota who were and are colleagues and friends, and to all of you, my readers.

Introduction

The world is rich with learning opportunities for children. And yet, our eagerness to expose children to the wonders of our technological society, coupled with our fears of ever-lurking strangers, means more children than ever before have never experienced the thrills of woods, fields, or streams, not to mention the very neighborhoods in which they live.

We owe it to the children we care for to take them out into their neighborhoods. Although books, computer images, videos, and film are all valid learning tools, they are all only two-dimensional, "virtual" experiences, and are no substitute for the real thing. And since young children have limited understanding of the world, they are unable to use these types of secondhand experiences and sources of information effectively. Children need to use all of their senses to gain an accurate and complete view of the world. This book is about fostering children's healthy development and enhancing children's learning experiences by extending their learning through a variety of different walking excursions that can be done simply by stepping out the door together.

Underlying Philosophies

To take full advantage of the learning opportunities inherent in new environments, many of the walks in this book suggest opportunities for children to use their senses of sight, hearing, smell, touch, and taste to experience the world firsthand. This involves slowing down and paying attention to details; it involves exploring with the children all of the things that are special about an outdoor space or indoor environment. As important, it involves using children's natural curiosity and wonder to help guide their learning.

This approach to young children's learning is most closely associated with emergent curriculum and Reggio-inspired curriculum, both of which emphasize developing and planning curriculum in response to children's interests and concerns. Unlike more traditional approaches to curriculum, which involve lesson plans with some type of "hook" intended to get children's attention, emergent curriculum and Reggio-inspired curriculum start by exploring what is engaging and meaningful to children. This does not mean you have no input or that there is no planning involved (see *Planning for the Walk*, page 5). In fact, you may have a general topic that children want to explore and may purposely include certain experiences as jumping-off points to spark their interests and challenge their thinking in some way. Setting the stage in this manner allows children to learn from their environment, as you arrange activities, structures, or objects that encourage discoveries and problem solving.

In Reggio-inspired programs, these jumping-off points, or planned opportunities for engagement, are called *provocations*. To set up meaningful provocations, use your knowledge of the children's prior experiences and learning as well as your observations of the children to help anticipate, shape, or guide the process. Look for moments when you can support children by asking open-ended questions, providing appropriate learning tools, sharing your own experiences or stories, and even helping seek the answers to questions. In emergent curriculum and Reggio-inspired curriculum, both adults and children have initiative and make decisions, which sets up a learning environment that is constantly evolving and diverging along new paths as choices and connections are made.

Another important component of Reggio-inspired and emergent curriculum has to do with documenting—showing and making visible—children's thinking and learning. *Documentation* focuses on and attempts to communicate the learning *process* to others; it is not about producing an end *product*. Documentation can take many forms, including photographs, recordings, transcripts, class murals, paintings and drawings, sculptures, and dramatic and literary creations, and often involves long-term projects consisting of multiple steps. The After the Walk section within each walking trip suggests ways of documenting the children's learning after the walk. However, these suggestions should not be interpreted as the only ways of showing children's developing thinking about the world.

Both emergent curriculum and Reggio-inspired curriculum involve flexibility and creativity on the part of the adults as well as an openness to seeing where the learning takes the children. And although this openness has its challenges, it also lends an element of excitement and desire that is at the very heart of learning.

Learning and Language

Learning and language go hand in hand. The development of language helps young children think, and developing new ways of thinking helps them learn language. For example, when learning the name of an object, a child must attend to the features that distinguish that object from others. Young children first learn to understand words that name specific objects or actions. Words that represent concepts or conditions (*big, round, soft*) rather than objects present more difficulty and only become understood through repeated exposure to those concepts in a variety of contexts. Hardest of all are words used to relate objects to each other, such as *underneath*, *behind*, or *over*. Children who have learned the names for relationships are better prepared to solve problems than other children.

You can aid in this process by providing children frequent and varied opportunities to talk and listen, such as supplying new vocabulary and encouraging them to generalize and state things in their own words. In addition, always provide good examples of language every time you interact with children.

Early Literacy Development

The early childhood years—from birth to age eight—are the most important period for literacy development. For children to be successful reading in school, they need to be engaged in experiences early on that build on prior learning and make future academic content meaningful (NAEYC and IRA 1998).

Birth through Preschool
Effective literacy instruction during the early years involves a variety of teaching strategies comprising developmentally appropriate environments, materials, experiences, and social support that will serve as the building blocks for conventional literacy instruction during children's later years. These teaching strategies include the following:

- rich adult talk, such as asking predictive and analytical questions and repeating new vocabulary frequently
- activities that increase children's awareness of the sounds of language (rhyme, alliteration, and sound matching)
- alphabet activities that promote identification of the letters of the alphabet
- support for emergent reading, for example, through well-designed library areas and literacy centers
- support for emergent writing, for example, by encouraging children to experiment with forming letters and invented spelling (Roskos, Christie, and Richgels 2003, 53–55)

However, the single most important thing you can do to build the skills essential for reading is to read aloud to children at least once or twice each day (NAEYC and IRA 1998). Remember that children's receptive language grows through continual exposure to a rich language environment and children's understanding of words and their meaning is often ahead of their ability to use those words. That ability grows through the encouragement and experiences adults provide to help children use their newly learned words.

Kindergarten and Early Elementary

Literacy instruction during kindergarten and early elementary should begin by observing and gauging where each child is developmentally and then building on that base. From there you can continue to employ some of the same teaching strategies used for younger groups, with an emphasis on print awareness and vocabulary development. Word walls, libraries rich with high-quality children's literature, and literacy centers that encourage letter identification and emergent writing skills are also important. Kindergarten, first, and second grade are also prime times to

capitalize on the active and social nature of children's learning through group dictation of stories and dramatic play experiences. The ability to read and write does not develop naturally, and children who have had regular and active interactions with print in their early years are far better prepared for the more formal literacy instruction they will encounter in school (NAEYC and IRA 1998).

How This Book Supports the Development of Language and Literacy

There are many activities you can do with children before, during, and after walks that support language and literacy development. For each of the walks in this book, any of the following activities can be implemented with the children. Use your knowledge of the children's abilities and level of development and modify the activities accordingly. More specific activities related to each walk's general theme are included in the After the Walk sections.

Before the Walk

Introduce the theme of the walk by sharing related books either gathered beforehand or gathered together with the children at a local library.

Invite a guest speaker (including family members) with knowledge related to the walk's theme to come speak to the children and answer any questions they may have. Afterward, write thank-you notes. Encourage younger children to contribute to a class thank-you note; encourage older children to write their own notes.

Invite the children to share their own experiences related to the topic of the walk. Ask, for example, "Who has ever visited a farm before?" "What did you see at the farm?" "Has anyone else ever seen piglets on a farm before?"

Introduce and reinforce vocabulary related to the theme, such as vocabulary from books and vocabulary mentioned by a guest speaker. Create a word wall that features the new vocabulary. For older children, create a group dictionary. Be sure to update the word wall and dictionary as children learn new vocabulary. Provide materials for children who want to keep individual dictionaries of the new words they learn.

Stage a *provocation*—a planned experience that will engage children and spark interest in the general focus of the walk. For example, for a rainy day walk, bring in items associated with the rain, such as umbrellas, rain coats, and rain boots. Or experiment with water using an eyedropper and a variety of materials, such as stones, feathers, grass, and leaves. Invite the children to drop water on each object and observe what happens.

Take the walk alone before walking with the children. Note opportunities to expand children's vocabulary and reinforce early literacy concepts, such as pointing out environmental print and asking open-ended questions.

During the Walk

Bring along a small notebook and list any new vocabulary mentioned. Be sure to use the new words during the walk as well.

Have children bring notebooks and writing and drawing tools with them on the walk. Invite children to draw pictures of or write about their experiences.

Point out and discuss environmental print, such as traffic-related signs and signs on buildings. Also watch for signs specifically related to the walk. For example, at a construction site, call children's attention to signs that read "Caution," "Danger," and "Restricted Area." Ask children to consider what the signs mean and why they are there.

If appropriate, ask people you encounter during the walk questions about what they are doing and why. At a home improvement store, for example, ask a person at the paint counter how paint colors are determined and how they are mixed.

Ask children to identify things, such as types of machinery at a construction site or items in the produce section at a grocery store.

Remember to sing songs, chant chants, and make up verses, such as "Oh, do you see the bird, the bird, as we are walking on" to help focus children's attention and aid in vocabulary building. Encourage the children to make up their own chants.

Ask open-ended questions to get children to extend their thinking, for example, "Why are some shadows big and others small?" and "What will happen to the leaves when the wind blows?"

After the Walk

Update a word wall or group dictionary with vocabulary from the walk as well as vocabulary that arises from the documentation process.

Write a book related to the walk, ensuring each child has an opportunity to contribute pages to it. Display the finished book for the children and their families to read.

Write thank-you notes to people who were especially helpful, such as a librarian or store manager. Be sure to mail the notes.

Re-create signs seen during the walks, such as "Children at play," "Do not enter," and "Quiet, please." Display them at the children's eye level.

Reread books related to the walk and discuss whether the things mentioned in the books were seen or experienced during the walk.

Invite older children to expand their learning by researching topics of interest from the walk. Children can then share their findings with others.

Planning for the Walk

Looking at the world through the eyes of a child can help you find valuable material for learning. Prior to walking with the children, go on the walk alone, paying attention to as many details as possible and to the ways your senses are activated. Thoughtful and purposeful planning will enable you to respond more quickly to the children's questions and discoveries. The ages of the children will determine the types of experiences that are appropriate for them to seek out during the walk.

Ask yourself the following questions beforehand to make the walk more meaningful and enjoyable and to ensure that the children are more easily guided.

- What things are the children already familiar with that relate to the new ideas, concepts, or experiences?
- What opportunities might I have or make to talk about the walk before, during, and after it?
- How can I encourage the children to talk about the walk before, during, and after it?
- In what ways can I expect the children to show their interest, reactions, or excitement on a particular walk? What can I do to reinforce these feelings?
- What secondary images (photographs, TV shows, videos, movies, books, displays) are available to reinforce the walk?
- What new social experiences will the children have and how can I plan to make them healthy experiences and opportunities for growth?
- What kinds of sensory experiences are available on the walk?
- What related experiences can I plan before and after the walk?

Keep in mind that for each walk, many more hidden learning experiences are bound to exist, and they often develop naturally and spontaneously from the children. Always allow children plenty of time to take their theories and ideas as far as possible. Sometimes this may last only a few days; sometimes the learning may become a long-term project that develops over many weeks. When children's projects are finished, carefully consider how you will display their work. This sends the message that you value their ideas and the expression of those ideas.

Walking with Children

The walks in this book are generally geared for children between birth and age eight. However, some walks may be more appropriate for older children. Use your knowledge of the children in your care as well as their interests before selecting walks.

Keeping the Children Safe

1. Take the children on a walk only after establishing good group control and the children have learned to remain with the group.
2. Arrange for extra help during the walk. When

establishing an adult-child ratio, consider the ages and personalities of the children. Keep in mind that children will benefit more from a walk if they can talk about their experiences with an adult and get answers to their questions. Here are suggested ratios:

- for children younger than two years old—one adult to one or two children, depending on the children's age; children who are not yet walking will likely require the full attention of one adult
- for children two years old—one adult to two children
- for children three years old—one adult to four children
- for children four and five years old—one adult to five children
- for school-age children—one adult to six or seven children

3. All adults should keep the following safety procedures in mind:
   - Be conscious at all times of the number of children you are responsible for and count heads frequently.
   - Concentrate on the children in your care and avoid being distracted by conversations with other adults.
   - Never leave children alone or send them ahead of the group for any reason. If necessary, for example, the whole group may need to go into a bathroom together.

4. Establish simple safety rules that are well known to all adults accompanying children. Help the children learn these rules by rehearsing or playing out the walk several days beforehand. Review the rules immediately before departing. Here are some sample safety rules:
   - Always wait for an adult before crossing streets or going into buildings.
   - Everyone hold hands near hazards.

- Always walk and never run.
- For groups of ten or more: "A leader in the front and a leader in the back and all the children in between." This is a helpful chant to use with younger children.

5. Bring along a first-aid kit on all walks. Tape an index card with emergency numbers to the top (including paramedics and poison control). Be sure the kit includes materials for cleaning scrapes and bruises; plenty of bandages; disposable nonporous, latex-free gloves; an instant cold pack; and any prescribed emergency medication needed for specific children (such as an epinephrine auto-injector). Bring the parent permission slips that include phone numbers where parents can be reached in an emergency or make a list of phone numbers for the kit.

6. Bring medications for children with allergies. Be sure to note whether any children are allergic to bee stings and have appropriate treatment.

7. Be sure all children are wearing tags that include the name and phone number of the center or care provider. For large groups, color code the tags so children and their group leader have tags of the same color. Do not put children's names on the tags.

8. When walking with very young children or in hazardous situations, use a knotted rope or looped walking rope as an added precautionary measure. Have each child hold on to a knot or loop on the rope.

9. Never leave a child alone or allow anyone to leave the group for any reason.

Walking with Toddlers
Because they are naturally curious and physically active, toddlers can present added challenges to a walk. Toddlers who are just learning to walk and are anxious to explore their world may find

it challenging to walk with a group. In addition, it is likely they will not know some of the basic safety precautions that older children do. Planning for safety is especially important for toddlers. If one or two toddlers are in a mixed-age group, they should be in a stroller or holding an adult's hand while walking. If traveling with a group of toddlers, a walking rope can be very helpful. This rope will have a knot or loop for each toddler to grasp and will provide security for the children and the adults who accompany them. Adults should carry all supplies in backpacks so both their hands are free.

Practicing before a walk can be helpful as well. For example, plan a brief walk around the outdoor play area to provide toddlers practice using a walking rope, following directions, and staying together. Decide on a word or words that tell everyone to immediately stop and listen. The words could be *freeze, statue, hands high,* or anything that becomes automatic for the children. When children hear the word or words, they should immediately freeze, make a statue, or stop and put their hands up high.

Walking with Children of All Ages

While walking along, consider singing songs to familiar tunes but changing the words to describe where the group is going and what the group will do there. (Older children may enjoy making up the lyrics themselves.)

Be sure to take photographs of the children as they engage in certain activities during the walk. Record the children asking questions or commenting on a discovery. Use the photographs and recordings afterward to help generate more discussions or as jumping-off points for projects and activities.

Finally, always remember to be flexible and ready to allow for exploration of things that attract the children's attention: the journey provides just as many opportunities for learning as does the destination.

Supporting Children Who May Be Anxious

Remember that children who are anxious in new situations and accept change reluctantly are apt to find a walk frightening or simply may not want to go. Such children need extra support, comfort, and individual attention on walks. These children should be with a familiar adult. Consider inviting adult family members to help ensure smooth experiences for these children. Volunteers should watch for signs that a child is becoming anxious and physically comfort that child. Also consider initially taking shorter walks to give the children time to become thoroughly familiar with the new setting and with the adults who care for them before venturing too far away.

Although the walking trips will provide a wealth of new experiences, these experiences can sometimes be frightening even to the most well-traveled child. Whenever possible, anticipate sounds and situations that might frighten children. (This is another reason why taking the walk prior to walking with children is good practice.) Prepare children for the walk by talking about potentially frightening things and perhaps even dramatizing them in advance. For example, you might say, "Some animals make loud noises. Let's all 'moo' as loud as we can to see what it might sound like at the farm we visit." These things can be done inside or during the walk, before encountering the potentially frightening thing. Discuss what to do if the sound occurs, such as cover ears, laugh, or jump two or three times. Although it is not possible to guess ahead of time what may frighten a particular child, it is worthwhile to identify some potentially frightening aspects and think of ways to prepare children for them.

Using This Book

All of the walks in this book require no transportation—only a pair of good walking shoes. Not all destinations will be within walking distance of every center or home where care is provided. Nonetheless, it is worth taking a look at all of the walks, since they all provide learning opportunities you can incorporate during or after other walks. Use the reproducible appendixes at the back of the book as you plan and implement your walking trips.

The walks themselves are grouped into three categories: Nature Walks, Community Walks, and Concept Walks. Each walking trip begins with a Before the Walk section that includes ideas to get children thinking about the upcoming walk, such as discussion topics, books to read, simple experiments, or jumping-off points (provocations). This section also includes a list of vocabulary words that may come up during the walk. You may choose only a few from the list to emphasize and explain, depending on the ages and developmental levels of the children. For example, the youngest children can learn new words when they are repeated frequently; three-year-olds can learn basic names of things and descriptive words; five-year-olds can learn more technical terms and words related to concepts. For older children, write the words on small pieces of paper or index cards so they can begin to recognize them. The vocabulary lists are not exhaustive. Incorporate additional words as they relate to your walking trip. Also consider presenting some words in a variety of languages. Translate words into languages spoken by the children in your care. Ask adult family members or older siblings to translate a few of the most common words on the list. Using words from different languages helps bridge language barriers, makes children more comfortable in a multilingual environment, and supports language learning.

This section also includes a list of suggested supplies to bring along on the walk (Things to Bring on the Walk), such as bags for collecting things, plastic magnifying glasses, and paper and pencils.

The During the Walk section includes ways children might use their senses to explore, activities children might do, and open-ended questions you might ask the children. Some walks include specific safety notes. Make sure to read these before starting out on the walk.

Since any experiences children have will make deeper impressions and last longer if they are reinforced, the After the Walk section suggests several activities to reinforce, extend, and document children's learning after they have returned from the walk. Many of the activities are related to language and literacy. Use the activities only if they are appropriate for the children's developmental levels and are interesting to them. Be prepared to adjust your plans or abandon activities that do not hold their interest or offer them challenges.

The Revisiting the Walk section offers ways of extending children's learning by repeating the walk or returning to the original destination and involving the people who work and play in the area. Or perhaps children will see something entirely different a second time that will take their learning to new places.

Finally, the book list in each walk contains a mix of old and new titles for various age groups. Some of the older titles are classics and may even have reissue dates. Many of the booklists include primarily nonfiction books. You can use them to present factual information on a particular topic.

The lists are by no means exhaustive and include just a sampling of what is available on any given topic. Many books series, such as the First Discovery Books, Let's Read and Find Out, Community Helpers, and so forth, are available and only a few titles from these series are included in some of the lists. Additional titles can be found on book covers or via the computer, and of course, your local librarian can help you find many suitable books on all of these topics. All of the books included here were available in our library system at the time of publication, but many children's books go out of print at a rapid rate. Fortunately, new books seem to appear at an equally rapid rate. Shopping library sales is a great way to build a library of your own on many of these timeless topics at a very reasonable cost.

References

National Association for the Education of Young Children (NAEYC) and International Reading Association (IRA). 1998. *Learning to read and write: Developmentally appropriate practices for young children.* Washington, DC: NAEYC. http://www.naeyc.org/about/positions/pdf/PSREAD98.PDF (accessed February 2009).

Roskos, Kathleen A., James F. Christie, and Donald J. Richgels. 2003. The essentials of early literacy instruction. *Young Children* 58 (2): 52–60. http://www.journal.naeyc.org/btj/200303.

Stacey, Susan. 2009. *Emergent curriculum in early childhood settings: From theory to practice.* St. Paul: Redleaf Press.

Wurm, Julianne. P. 2005. *Working in the Reggio way: A beginner's guide for American teachers.* St. Paul: Redleaf Press.

Nature Walks

"A rain shower on a stream with a purple butterfly"
Victoria, age 7

Cold Day Walk

Before the Walk

Children constantly use their senses to learn—in fact, for young children, all learning is sensory based: a baby puts everything in her mouth; a toddler touches and moves everything; and a preschooler asks a million questions. All are learning through their senses. As children develop the cognitive processes to sort through this learning and the language to talk about it, they organize the learning into knowledge and useful groupings. A major part of this sorting process takes place during the preschool years. For school-age children, focusing attention on using particular senses can expand their knowledge base and enhance language development as they are challenged to use their senses to gather information and then communicate their findings to others. Sensory walks, such as a walk that encourages children to explore the concept of *cold*, are beneficial to children of all ages. A cold day walk gives children an opportunity to

- **experience how cold feels**
- **observe the effects of cold weather on animals, plants, water, and other things in the environment**
- **notice steam, smoke, and their breath**

Depending on the ages of the children in your group, your cold day walk may focus on any number of things related to cold, for example, how the cold affects plants and living creatures, how we know it's cold outside (frost, ice, bare trees, fewer wild creatures), and how colors and light are different when it's cold outside. Of course, your walk will also be affected by the climate in which you live—if you live in a warm climate, the signs of cold weather may be more subtle.

Prior to walking with the children, talk about the concept of cold. For younger children, set up a table with a variety of cold or cool items for them to touch as well as items that are warm or room temperature. Include things such as a bowl of ice cubes and a bowl of soapy, warm water. Invite the children to tell you what things are cold and what things are not cold. Older children might enjoy reading books about weather, such as books that explain what makes weather. Or consider inviting a weather professional to show occupational tools and materials.

Words to Use and Learn

chill	freezing level	harden	temperature
chilly	frigid	ice	thermometer
cold	frost	icy	32 degrees
freeze	frostbite	shiver	tremble
freezing	frozen	solid	windchill

Things to Bring on the Walk

✓ a spiral notebook that includes the children's questions and notes about experiences that might interest them (provocations), and for noting your observations of the children during the walk

✓ backpacks or paper bags for collecting things

✓ writing and drawing tools

✓ a camera

✓ a tape recorder or other recording device

✓ small hammers or other tools for breaking or cracking ice

✓ small, unbreakable objects or toys for sliding on frozen puddles or sidewalks

 **During the Walk**

While you walk with the children, pay attention to details and encourage children to use their own observational skills. Ask open-ended questions to challenge their thinking and present more opportunities for exploration. Respond to the children's questions and observations in a thoughtful manner, which can include answering a question with a question.

Invite older children to walk silently for five minutes, using their senses of sight, hearing, and touch to make observations about cold weather. While they walk, have them stop to write or draw pictures of what they see, hear, and touch. At the end of five minutes, have the children share some of their observations with others. Do the children think they saw, heard, and felt more while they walked in silence than if they had talked the whole time? Why or why not?

👁 Using the Sense of Sight

What are the colors of "cold"? What color is the sky? What colors are the trees and plants? What color is the ground? What colors are the children's own hands and faces?

Are there shadows? What do they look like? Do shadows change with the seasons?

How does the cold affect plants and trees? Are their petals and leaves gone? Are they shriveled? Is there ice on the leaves or branches?

Are there clouds in the sky? Does the number of clouds in the sky affect how cold it is outside?

What does frozen water look like?

What happens to people's breath when it's cold outside? Why?

Using the Sense of Hearing

How are sounds in nature affected by the cold? Are there more sounds? Are the sounds sharper or more clear? Do the sounds travel farther?

Are tree branches breaking from the weight of ice or because the sun is melting the ice, which is falling to the ground?

Are there sounds from vehicle tires slipping or skidding on the ice?

Using the Sense of Touch

Can you tell by looking at things how cold they are? Are some things colder than others? For example, is a mailbox colder than a tree branch?

Can you tell by touching ice on a puddle how thick it is? Can the ice be broken by a light tap or is it difficult to break?

Why do some things freeze or ice over and some things do not?

Are there degrees of cold? Which things are very cold, which are medium cold, and which are not so cold? One way to test degrees of cold might be for children to see how long they can hold their hand on something before it becomes uncomfortable.

Where Have the Birds and Animals Gone?

Are there fewer birds and animals when it's cold outside? What do animals do when it's cold? Where do they go? Encourage children to speculate which animals may be hibernating inside trees or underground, and which may have flown off for warmer climates. Older children can make a list of the creatures who are missing and where they might have gone.

Exploring Ice

Invite children to explore ice in a puddle, on a sidewalk, or even as an icicle. How would they describe ice? How does ice feel? Is it cold? Smooth? Slippery? What does ice look like? What color is ice? As younger children describe ice, write down their thoughts in your notebook. Have older children think about how they would describe ice and write their thoughts down on paper.

Ice Is Slippery

Have children slide small, unbreakable objects or toys on frozen puddles or sidewalks. Invite children to wonder why ice is slippery. What about ice makes it slippery? Does everything slide on ice? Experiment with sliding several objects on ice. Do leaves slide on ice? Does a mitten slide on ice? Do sticks slide on ice? What about small stones? Then ask the children to share characteristics of things that do and do not slide on ice.

What Is Affected by the Cold?

Invite children to notice or collect items that are affected by the cold or that look different in colder weather. Are all natural things affected? What happens to trees in the cold? What happens to the ground? Are stones affected by the cold? Are sidewalks affected by the cold? Make a list with the children of all the things affected by cold weather.

 **After the Walk**

Sometimes after a walk it is helpful to gather the children briefly to discuss observations and share items collected during the walk. Refer to your notes, if needed, to remind children about events or questions that generated the most interest. Use these to help children think of ways they might choose to document their learning during the walk.

Older Children

School-age children are likely to come up with a number of ways to express their learning during the walk in the cold. Did any children comment on the difference in colors during the walk? For example, was the scenery dominated by darker, "cooler" tones? If so, invite the children to identify those colors and then paint pictures using only a "cold-weather palette." Besides paint tones, what other materials might children use to convey the feeling of colder weather? For example, metal can convey a starkness or coldness that other materials cannot. Encourage children who are interested in creating three-dimensional works to consider using metallic materials such as wire to construct barren and frozen trees.

If you asked the older children in your group to note their observations of the cold during a silent five-minute walk, have them write about their experiences. Would their observations have been different if they had been allowed to talk with one another? How?

Create a class thesaurus with *cold* as the first entry. How many other words are there for cold?

Have children create a weather station for observing, recording, and reporting the weather. Children can create their own book of weather words to use for specific types of weather conditions.

If children wondered where certain wild creatures went during cold weather, have them research the animals or birds and report their findings to the class.

Younger Children

Younger children can continue learning about cold through more sensory-related activities. For example, children might identify other things as feeling like ice or looking like ice, such as cellophane, foil, mirrored tile pieces, or sheets of metal. Bring in a collection of materials for children to use to create displays of other things that make them think of ice.

Invite the children to use the items they collected to show how things change (or don't change) with the cold season.

Add new words related to cold to an existing word wall, including other words that mean cold.

Make a class book about ice that includes real items children have identified as looking like or feeling like ice. Children can also create their own books about ice.

Have children begin their own Opposites Books, beginning with the opposites *cold* and *hot*. Children can think of things they saw during the walk that demonstrated cold and draw pictures of them in their books. Have children add to their Opposites Books as new concepts about opposites are explored.

What do we wear when it's cold? To help children with vocabulary development, collect a variety of cold-weather fabric scraps, such as wool, faux fur, and fleece. Discuss with the children the different types of clothing people wear when it's cold outside as well as the fabrics most often used to create the clothes. Have children examine the fabric scraps and describe them.

Revisiting the Walk

Throughout the winter months, each time you take the children on a walk, ask them whether the current day is colder than or not as cold as the previous days you went walking together. How can they tell? Did they wear a coat and hat the last time they went for a walk? Are they wearing a coat and hat this time? Is the season about to change? What things tell them that a different season may be approaching?

Books

Chambers, Catherine. 2002. *Big freeze*. Chicago: Heinemann Library.

Dahl, Michael, and Brian Jensen. 2006. *Cold, colder, coldest: Animals that adapt to cold weather*. Minneapolis: Picture Window Books.

Frost, Helen. 2000. *Water as a solid*. Mankato, MN: Pebble Books.

Gibbons, Gail. 1990. *Weather words and what they mean*. New York: Holiday House.

Holland, Gini. 2008. *Hot and cold*. Milwaukee, WI: Weekly Reader Early Learning Library.

Kuskin, Karla, and Fumi Kosaka. 2004. *Under my hood I have a hat*. New York: Laura Geringer Books.

Lamb, Albert, and David McPhail. 2006. *Sam's winter hat*. New York: Scholastic.

Lilly, Melinda, and Scott M. Thompson. 2006. *Water and ice*. Vero Beach, FL: Rourke Publishing.

Peters, Lisa Westberg, and Sam Williams. 2000. *Cold little duck, duck, duck*. New York: Greenwillow Books.

Royston, Angela. 2002. *Hot and cold*. Chicago: Heinemann Library.

Rustad, Martha E. H. 2006. *Today is cold*. Mankato, MN: Capstone Press.

Saunders-Smith, Gail. 1998. *Warm clothes*. Mankato, MN: Pebble Books.

Schaefer, Lola M., and Gail Saunders-Smith. 2000. *A cold day*. Mankato, MN: Pebble Books.

Stringer, Lauren. 2006. *Winter is the warmest season*. Orlando: Harcourt.

Hot Day Walk

Before the Walk

For young children, using their senses is one way they learn fundamental skills and concepts. Young children learn best when they can control and act upon their environment. Walks that invite them to think about and explore concepts as basic as *hot* do much to enhance their understanding of the world around them. For older children, the benefits include being outdoors and experiencing things firsthand, rather than on a TV or video screen. There is also something to be said for simply having children slow down and pay attention to the smaller details of the world around them, such as how warm the weather is and how warm weather affects different things in the environment. A walk exploring the concept of *hot* provides an opportunity to

- observe firsthand how the sun or shade affects how warm or hot it feels

- notice the effect of heat on various materials, objects, and vegetation

- conduct experiments on how things react to being exposed to heat

- experience different types of heat-related weather, such as dry, humid, windy, or still

- consider the ways people respond to heat and how they protect themselves and their environment

Prior to walking with the children, talk about the concept of *hot*. Even very young children are likely to have heard the word *hot*, perhaps as a warning by an adult such as "Watch out! It's hot!" or "Let's test the bath water to make sure it isn't too hot." Find out what the children in your group know about *hot*. Some children may need to be reassured that it is okay to observe and talk about hot things, such as hot weather, and that you will not ask them to touch things that are not safe.

Words to Use and Learn

boil	heat	humidity	sunshine
burn	heat stroke	melt	temperature
dehydrate	heat wave	sun	thermometer
dry	hot	sunburn	tropical
evaporate	humid	sunscreen	warm

Things to Bring on the Walk

✓ a spiral notebook that includes the children's questions and notes about experiences that might interest them (provocations), and for noting your observations of the children during the walk

✓ sunglasses and hats

✓ backpacks or paper bags for collecting things

✓ a camera

✓ a tape recorder or other recording device

✓ writing and drawing tools

✓ water bottles or other containers for holding drinking water and water to use for experiments

✓ items that melt easily, such as small pieces of chocolate

✓ measuring tools such as tape measures, rulers, or string

✓ sidewalk chalk

During the Walk

At the beginning of the walk, take a few minutes to walk quietly, encouraging the children to use their senses to help them learn more about how the heat affects the things around them as well as themselves. How do they feel after walking a while in the heat?

Children of all ages can be encouraged to use their senses to experience hot weather and the effect of the hot weather on the environment.

👁 Using the Sense of Sight

How are colors in the natural world affected by heat? Are they brighter or more intense? Are they so bright they appear almost white? Do the children have to put on sunglasses to see certain things?

Are there shadows? What do they look like? Do they change according to the time of day?

How does the heat affect flowers, plants, and trees? Do their petals and leaves droop or curl under? Why?

Can heat be seen rising from the pavement or the hoods of cars? What does it look like? Where else can heat be seen rising?

What color is the sky? Are there clouds in the sky? Does the number of clouds affect the temperature?

Can the children tell how hot things might be by looking at them? How?

Are there many people walking about? Are there any animals such as dogs or birds?

🦻 Using the Sense of Hearing

How are sounds in the environment affected by the heat? Does it seem quieter or louder?

Are there any animal sounds, such as dogs barking?

What sounds might indicate it's a hot day? Do the children hear any sprinklers or people washing their cars?

Using the Sense of Touch

Can the children tell by looking at things how warm or hot they are, such as car hoods or sidewalks? Are some things hotter than others? Why?

Do some materials or colors soak up the heat more than others? Which ones?

Can the children feel a breeze in the air? Is the breeze warm or cool? Is the temperature more pleasant with a slight breeze?

Does It Melt?

Invite the children to explore which things melt quickly in hot weather and which things do not. Find a sunny area and set out a few items you brought that will melt fairly rapidly. Also set out a few items that won't melt, such as pebbles or small sticks. Continue the walk. Just prior to going back inside, check on the items and ask the children what happened while they were away. Did any of the items melt? Which ones did not melt?

Evaporation

Find a paved area near the center where you can pour some water to create a few puddles both in the sun and in the shade. Help the children use the sidewalk chalk to draw outlines of the puddles. Children can also use the string to measure the perimeters of the puddles. Have the children check the puddles throughout the day and note any changes. Discuss any changes in the puddles, including which puddles are evaporating the quickest and why.

Hot-Color Names

Colors can be identified as "hot" or "cool" as well as by the feelings or emotions they evoke. Ask the children to notice which colors around them appear to be hot. Do some colors appear hotter than others? Have the children help create a list of all the hot colors they see and then create new names for the colors. For example, the children may notice several shades of red, all of which they call hot. What names can they think of for the different reds that might indicate their degree of hotness? If one red appears hotter than another, perhaps the hottest red is called "too-hot-to-touch red" while the other is a warmer "tomato-soup red." Consider continuing naming colors after the walk too.

 **After the Walk**

Remind the children of how they used their senses of sight, hearing, and touch to explore the concept of *hot* during the walk. Ask what they learned about *hot* and what *hot* means to them. What did they learn from the experiments they conducted?

Older Children

The act of slowing down to observe things in the environment may have been a new experience for some older children. If this is the case, ask open-ended questions as a way of encouraging children to share their experiences. For example, ask whether it is possible to explain a hot day without ever having experienced one. Invite children to use all of the descriptive words they can think of to describe a hot day to someone who has never experienced a hot day before. Suggest that they begin by describing what a hot day looks like, what a hot day sounds like, and what a hot day feels like. Afterward, ask them if it is truly possible to experience something without firsthand knowledge. How does experiencing something add to your overall understanding of it? Invite children to create color charts of hot colors using crayons or colored pencils. Encourage children to blend colors to create new ones they may have observed outside. Point out that the names of colors are written on crayons and tubes of acrylic and oil paints. Wonder who invented all of the color names and when. Then have the children name all of the colors on their hot-colors chart.

Why do shadows grow longer or shorter? Why do their outlines become more defined or less defined? Have children research shadows and then create posters illustrating and explaining the changes in shadows.

Sunbathe, Sunbelt, sunburn, sunflower, Sunday . . . How many words can the children think of that include the word *sun*? Have the children make a list of all the sun words they can think of. Then challenge them to use all of the sun words in a story or poem.

Invite children to create different types of poems about the sun or heat, such as acrostic poems. Acrostic poems begin with a word such as *sunshine* or *evaporate* that is written vertically on a sheet of paper. Then use each letter of the word to start a new sentence or phrase that is related to the word. An acrostic poem for the word *sunny* might look like this:

SUNNY
So hot
Under the tree
No cool breeze anywhere
No relief
Yet the forecast said "Rain"!

Younger Children
Which activity or activities did the children seem to enjoy most during the walk? One way to initiate

a discussion is to show them the photos you took and ask, "What were you doing in this picture?" You will be able to tell based on the children's descriptions which ones held their interest the most. Then think about how children might extend their learning through a related project, either individually or with a small group. For example, read books or talk with the children about shadows. What are shadows? Does everyone have a shadow? Where do shadows go at night? Why are shadows always black? Create an area inside dedicated to shadows and include children's dictation and shadow artwork they create.

Add new words related to heat and the sun on an existing word wall or a weather word wall.

Sing songs or perform fingerplays about the sun. Can the children make up their own songs or fingerplays about the sun?

Have the children begin Opposites Books. Talk with the children about opposites, such as hot and cold, black and white, over and under, big and small. The first page could be a hot-and-cold page. Invite children to draw pictures of things that are hot and things that are cold. Continue to have children create other pages of opposites. After a few weeks, help the children assemble their Opposites Books. Then invite each child to share his or her book of opposites with the group.

What is hot and what is not? Have the children help you identify things in the room that are hot or not hot. Write *hot* and *not hot* on several index cards. Then work with the children to tape the labels to the appropriate areas or things in the room that are hot and not hot. This is a good time to review safety rules concerning hot things as well.

Revisiting the Walk

Throughout the summer months, each time you take the children on a walk, ask them whether the current day is hotter than or not as hot as the previous days you went walking together. How can they tell? Did they wear a sweater the last time they went for a walk? Are they wearing a sweater this time? Is the season about to change? What things tell them that a different season may be approaching?

Books

Auch, Alison. 2002. *That's hot!* Minneapolis: Compass Point Books.

Bailey, Jacqui, and Matthew Lilly. 2004. *Sun up, sun down: The story of day and night.* Minneapolis: Picture Window Books.

Claybourne, Anna. 2001. *Summer.* North Mankato, MN: Thameside Press.

Crews, Nina. 1995. *One hot summer day.* New York: Greenwillow Books.

Dahl, Michael, and Brian Jensen. 2006. *Hot, hotter, hottest: Animals that adapt to great heat.* Minneapolis: Picture Window Books.

English, Karen, and Javaka Steptoe. 2004. *Hot day on Abbott Avenue.* New York: Clarion Books.

Fandel, Jennifer. 2003. *Heat.* Mankato, MN: Smart Apple Media.

Hewitt, Sally. 2000. *Hot and cold.* New York: Children's Press.

Hidalgo, Maria. 2007. *Heat.* Mankato, MN: Creative Education.

Lilly, Melinda, and Scott M. Thompson. 2006. *Hot and cold.* Vero Beach, FL: Rourke Publishing.

Mack, Lorrie. 2004. *Weather.* New York: Dorling Kindersley.

Marzollo, Jean, and Laura Regan. 1997. *Sun song.* London: HarperCollins World.

Stille, Darlene R., and Sheree Boyd. 2004. *Temperature: Heating up and cooling down.* Minneapolis: Picture Window Books.

Thomas, Rick, and Denise Shea. 2005. *Sizzle! A book about heat waves.* Minneapolis: Picture Window Books.

Trumbauer, Lisa. 2003. *All about heat.* New York: Children's Press.

Rainy Day Walk

Before the Walk

Children are fascinated with water. A rainy day walk exposes children to a variety of sensory experiences and can easily stimulate long-term project work. Rain is a critical component of the Earth's ecosystem and can be a lot of fun to explore. A walk in a soft rain, or just after a rain, allows children an opportunity to

- notice the effects of rain
- learn about puddles and where they form
- observe where water goes and how it moves
- float small items in rivulets of water and experiment with sinking and floating
- observe worms
- consider the importance of rain
- look for a rainbow

Prior to the walk, read several stories to very young children about rain and rainy days to establish a knowledge base and to excite them about the walk. Invite the children to share their experiences with rain. Have they even been caught in a rainstorm? What happened? Talk about why it rains and what would happen if it never rained.

Some children may need to be reassured that it is okay to walk in a soft rain, and that you will keep them safe. Introduce the things you plan to bring for the walk and suggest ways children might use them.

Words to Use and Learn

absorb	earthworm	monsoon	raincoat
clouds	evaporate	mud	storm
damp	fog	puddle	thunder
drain	lightning	rain	umbrella
drizzle	moisture	rainbow	wet

Things to Bring on the Walk

✓ a spiral notebook that includes the children's questions and notes about experiences that might interest them (provocations), and for noting your observations of the children during the walk

✓ backpacks or paper bags for collecting things

✓ writing and drawing tools

✓ objects for floating and sinking experiments in puddles, such as small toy boats, leaves, stones, rocks, twigs, bottle caps, pennies, nails, and craft foam

✓ towels for drying hands and feet

✓ a camera

✓ a tape recorder or other recording device

During the Walk

Remember to slow down and follow the children's lead. Pay attention to details and work to fine-tune the children's observational skills as well. Be on the alert for creating moments that will surprise and delight the children. Ask open-ended questions to enhance their learning and to present more possibilities for exploration. Your role is to spark the children's interest and curiosity. Use the following suggestions or come up with some of your own based on your knowledge of the children in your group.

As you and the children walk before, after, or even during a light rain shower, encourage them to use all of their senses to investigate and explore what is special about rain. Always take care to tailor your questions and the activities to the developmental level of the children in your group.

👁 Using the Sense of Sight

How do the sky and the light change when it rains? Is it darker just before a rain shower? Is it lighter after a rain shower?

How do the reflections from puddles affect the light and color all around them?

What does the rain look like as it falls? Where does the water go?

How does the rain affect flowers, plants, and trees? Do their petals or branches droop? Do the rain droplets form small pools inside flowers or buds? Where else does the water collect?

Is there a rainbow in the sky? What are the colors of a rainbow? What causes rainbows?

Using the Sense of Smell

What are the different smells in the air? What does it mean when people say, "It smells like rain"? Can you really smell rain? Are the smells different before, after, and during a rain shower?

What do puddles smell like? What does mud smell like? What do wet flowers and plants smell like?

Using the Sense of Hearing

How are sounds in nature affected by an imminent rain shower? Are the birds quieter? Are their calls different?

How are sounds in nature different just after a rain shower? Are the birds noisier? Are their calls different?

What does rain sound like? What does thunder sound like?

What other sounds can the children hear?

Using the Sense of Taste

What does the rain taste like as it falls on the children's tongues? Can children catch the rain in their cupped hands and taste it?

What would a "recipe" for rain include as its main ingredients?

Using the Sense of Touch

What do different things such as cars, sidewalks, and toys left in the rain feel like when they are wet?

Depending on the weather and other conditions, consider inviting children to remove their socks and shoes and walk barefoot in the grass or in small puddles. What does wet grass feel like on their feet? What do puddles feel like on their feet?

Rainwater

Look for places where the water is flowing. What makes the water move? Have the children put some twigs in the flowing water to see what happens. Or put a large rock in the twig's path. What are some ways to stop the water from flowing?

Watch the water flow down a sewer drain. Where does the water go from there?

Worms

Look for worms and observe them. Have children dig in the soil to see if there are any worms. Are there more worms on the sidewalks or in the soil? What happens to worms left on the sidewalk?

Does It Sink or Float?

Float the objects you brought along in the puddles and little streams formed after a rain shower. Notice which things float and which don't. Collect the things that float in one container and the things that don't in another. Guess what makes things float.

After the Walk

Back inside, children's discoveries, collected items, and theories can become the starting point for documenting what they know or think about rain. Refer to your notes, if needed, to remind, inspire, and excite children about some aspect of the rainy day walk. Remember that your role is to facilitate children's learning.

Older Children

Discuss possible ways of documenting the walk, such as paintings, drawings, clay or paper sculptures, wire constructions, transparent collages that color the light, mobiles, and illustrated stories or poems.

If some children want to work together, they might consider making a group mural of a rainy-day scene for a wall in the room that includes 3-D items such as cotton balls, tin foil, clear plastic, and fabric scraps.

Make a pro and con chart about rain. Have children finish the sentences "I like rain because . . ." and "I don't like rain because . . ."

Choose a word listed in Words to Use and Learn on page 30. Write the word on chart paper. Have children make up as many words as they can using the letters in the selected word.

Invite children to write acrostic poems about rain. Acrostic poems begin with a word such as *thunder* or *umbrella* written vertically on a sheet of paper. Then use each letter of the word to start a new sentence or phrase that is related to the word.

For example, using the word *rain*, an acrostic poem might look like this:

RAIN
Really wet
And cold outside
Inside it's
Nice and dry and warm

Print photographs taken during the walk. Children can use the photographs to make a class book about the rainy day walk.

Younger Children

Younger children may simply delight in splashing in and experimenting with water at the sensory table, in which case you might take photos or make audio recordings of them at play.

Reinforce new words by adding them to an existing word wall. Remember to use the words again on the next rainy day.

Introduce rhyming by asking children what rhymes with *rain*, *wet*, or *mud*. Add the new rhyming words to the word wall.

Reread books about rain that were read previously.

Print photographs taken during the walk. Glue them inside a blank book and have children write or draw anything they like next to the photographs.

Revisiting the Walk

Plan to take the same walk again on another rainy day to observe new things, to test theories, or even to be reminded of rainy-day colors and light. Consider involving people who work or play in the area. Work with the children to generate a list of the people they are likely to see. What questions might the children ask them or what might the children want to observe the people doing?

Books

Bauer, Marion Dane, and John Wallace. 2004. *Rain*. New York: Aladdin.

Branley, Franklyn Mansfield, and James Graham Hale. 1997. *Down comes the rain*. New York: HarperCollins Publishers.

Burke, Jennifer S. 2000. *Rainy days*. New York: Children's Press.

Grazzini, Francesca, and Chiara Carrer. 1996. *Rain, where do you come from?* Brooklyn, NY: Kane/Miller Book Publishers.

Hest, Amy, and Jill Barton. 1999. *In the rain with Baby Duck*. Cambridge, MA: Candlewick Press.

Jacobs, Marian B. 1999. *Why does it rain?* New York: PowerKids Press.

Laser, Michael, and Jeffrey Greene. 1997. *The rain*. New York: Simon & Schuster Books for Young Readers.

Llewellyn, Claire, and Anthony Lewis. 1995. *Wind and rain*. Hauppauge, NY: Barron's.

Milbourne, Anna, Sarah Gill, Laura Fearn, and Laura Parker. 2005. *The rainy day*. Tulsa, OK: EDC.

Miles, Elizabeth. 2005. *Rain*. Chicago: Heinemann Library.

Nelson, Robin. 2002. *A rainy day*. Minneapolis: Lerner Publications.

Rustad, Martha E. H. 2006. *Today is rainy*. Mankato, MN: Capstone Press.

Saunders-Smith, Gail. 1999. *Rain*. Mankato, MN: Pebble Books.

Stewart, Melissa, and Constance Rummel Bergum. 2008. *When rain falls*. Atlanta: Peachtree.

Ward, Kristin. 2000. *Rain*. New York: PowerKids Press.

Windy Day Walk

Before the Walk

Most children have felt the wind blow in their faces, but otherwise have little information about the wind. Using your knowledge of the children, consider which aspects of the wind might peak their interests most. A windy day offers many new areas for exploration, learning, and opportunities to

- **notice how the wind moves and transports things, such as leaves, dirt, and paper**

- **observe the effect of the wind on different things indoors and outdoors, such as trees, puddles, windows, and doors**

- **feel the wind in different places and from different directions**

- **consider what wind is and how we measure it**

- **look for wind-related objects, such as weather vanes, kites, and pinwheels**

- **learn how weather is forecasted and how to understand weather reports**

For very young children, consider calling their attention to the wind during outdoor playtimes. Why is their hair blowing across their faces and making it hard for them to see? Can they make the wind cease by going behind a big tree or play structure? Make note of these conversations and any ideas for extending children's learning about the wind during the walk. For example, did any children take delight in "hiding from the wind"? Were they fascinated by the way the wind came in gusts and shook the trees and scattered the leaves?

Older children might want to know where the wind comes from and how it is measured. Consider sharing books about the wind as well as actual items that measure the wind, for example, weather vanes and wind socks. Invite the children to watch weather reports on TV and note some of the things always mentioned, such as storm fronts and high- and low-pressure areas. Do the reports mention the wind? Do they mention wind direction or wind speed?

Words to Use and Learn

blowing	high	pressure	whirlwind
blustery	hurricane	prevailing	wind
breeze	knots	tornado	windchill
breezy	low	weather vane	windmill
gale	meteorologist	whirl	wind speed

Things to Bring on the Walk

✔ a spiral notebook that includes the children's questions and notes about experiences that might interest them (provocations), and for noting your observations of the children during the walk

✔ a camera

✔ notebooks for the children

✔ writing and drawing tools

✔ backpacks or paper bags for collecting things

✔ flags, balloons, pinwheels, and different kinds of kites

✔ bubble-blowing liquid and wands

✔ Frisbee flying toys

✔ balls of different weights (beach balls, sponge balls, whiffle balls, and rubber balls)

✔ wind-related items such as weather vanes, anemometers, streamers, wind skippers, parachutes, and paper planes. You can download instructions for making these and other wind-sensitive items from the Redleaf Web site, www.redleafpress.org. Enter "Hey Kids!" into the search field and follow the links.

During the Walk

Consider using some of the following suggestions during the walk to help children observe the effects of the wind. Should children discover other aspects of the wind that interest them, be sure to help them pursue and later document those interests.

👁 Using the Sense of Sight

Look at the trees for any signs of the wind. Are the leaves and branches moving? Do they move more at the top of the tree or near the bottom? Are some trees moving and some not moving?

Notice how the wind affects flowers, plants, and shrubs. Does the thickness of the leaves or clusters of branches make any difference? Which plants seem most affected by the wind? What does wind do to some of the flower petals?

Does the location of the trees and plants make any difference in terms of how the wind affects them? Do things blow around more if they are out in the open or up against a building or wall? Do they blow more on one side of the building or the other side? Wonder why that might be and whether it would always be the same.

What other parts of trees and plants are blown by the wind? Are seeds or fluff from plant life being transported by the wind? Where do they land? Look for things children could observe to see how the wind will affect them, such as dandelion fluff, silk from milkweed pods, cotton fluff from trees, and other seeds.

How does the wind affect other objects in the environment? For example, dust or debris along the walk; raindrops or water from sprinklers, in puddles, or in ponds; smoke or steam from chimneys; flags; hanging planters, hanging lights, or wind chimes.

Are the clouds moving quickly or slowly?

Is the wind blowing people's clothing, their hair, or items they are holding or using?

Using the Sense of Sight (Continued)

Let the children hold any wind toys you brought along and observe what happens. Have them hold the toys in several different positions and directions to observe the wind's effect. Blow bubbles in the wind and see what happens to them.

 Using the Sense of Smell

Does the wind produce any special aromas? Are there any strong aromas such as smoke? Are cooking aromas stronger on a windy day?

Using the Sense of Hearing

Listen to the sounds related to the wind. Ask the children what sounds they hear: leaves rustling, objects flapping, whistling, or humming. Do they hear any wind chimes? Decide whether the wind makes the sounds or whether the things the wind is moving make the sounds. Do the sounds get louder, softer, or change in any way? What contributes to those changes?

Have the children shout into the wind to see what happens to their voices. Are they as loud as usual? Can they hear each other in the wind?

Can the children imitate the sounds of the wind?

Using the Sense of Touch

Can the children feel the wind? Is it cool or warm? Are there any gritty textures from dust?

Using Wind-Related Objects and Toys

If you brought along wind objects or toys, have the children use them to explore the qualities of the wind.

Use the weather vane to find the direction of the wind. Does the wind's direction stay constant or does it change? Repeat this on different windy day walks, recording the wind's direction.

Use the anemometer to see how fast the wind is blowing. Count the number of times the spoons rotate in one minute and use that as your own measurement of wind speed. Repeat this several times to see whether the wind speed is the same or if it changes. Take some measurements when the wind is gusting and discuss what that might mean.

Have the children try holding different items in the wind, such as flags, balloons, pinwheels, and different kinds of kites. See what happens. On a very windy day, hold up white strips of textured cloth, such as terry cloth, to see if they pick up any dust from the wind. Do they catch other objects, such as seeds, blowing in the wind?

Have the children experiment with objects of different weights to see how the wind affects them.

What happens to things like balloons, feathers, papers, rocks, and blocks when they are left in the wind? Try tossing homemade parachutes around to see what the wind does to them. Try throwing Frisbees and balls of different weights. Does the wind have any effect on where they go or land? Practice flying paper and Styrofoam planes.

Sketching a Windy Day

Some children may want to use the notebooks and drawing tools to sketch what things look like on a windy day. How does the strength of the wind affect objects such as trees, plants, and flags? How does the strength of the wind affect how people move and get around? For children who enjoy drawing, suggest they make sketches of the same objects in the same location on different days to compare the effects of the wind on those objects.

Photographs in the Wind

Take photographs of the children and how they explore on a windy day. Be sure to capture children engaged in what interests them most. Photographs can be especially helpful back inside when children begin documenting their experiences with the wind.

After the Walk

Help the children assemble things they may have collected on the walk. Discuss ideas that interest them about the wind. Notice which things or concepts seem particularly compelling and use them as starting points for assisting children in documenting their various routes of thinking. Share the digital photos with the children or print copies as soon as possible.

Older Children

Older children have a greater knowledge base and can think more abstractly about subjects such as the wind. This will also be evident in the many ways they choose to document their learning. Did a child draw sketches of the wind over several days? Did a child who was fascinated by the windy weather decide to create a weather station and report on the weather each day? A child with an interest in the performing arts might enjoy seeing the video of the mime artist Marcel Marceau pretending to walk on a very windy day and creating his own pantomime version of walking against a gale.

Invite children to create poems titled "Windy Walk." See how many words they can use in their poems that begin with the letter W.

Many stories involve events related to the wind or weather, such as *Winnie the Pooh and the Blustery Day*. Have children create their own stories or dramas that involve the weather.

Have children consider the question, "What would we do without wind?" Work with the children to create a list of all the things that depend on the power of the wind, such as sailboats, hang gliders, kites, windmills, wind turbines, and wind surfers.

Have children create Wind Journals by documenting the wind for seven days. For each day, have them create their own words to describe the wind, such as "hair-in-your-eyes wind," "flag-fluttering wind," and "come-and-go wind." Encourage them to create a glossary of their new wind words at the end of the journal.

Younger Children

Since young children are such tactile learners, it is possible they may have collected a number of items from the walk or simply enjoyed experimenting with the items you brought along. Perhaps a child is fascinated with the power of the wind to shake tree branches and fold over flowers. How could a child use art materials to show or help explain wind power? Could wires be bent in the shape of drooping flowers? Which fabrics might best replicate the flapping of a flag against a flag pole? As you listen to a child describe her experiences with the wind, be thinking of ways to enhance or help the child expand her theories.

Add new words related to wind or the weather to an existing word wall.

Read books related to the wind and weather. Compare the weather in the books to the current day's weather or the weather observed during the walk.

Create a class book called "Our Windy Walk." Invite each child to draw a picture of a windy day to add to the book. Place the book in the library or literacy center when it is complete.

Purchase or make recordings of the wind for children to listen to. Ask the children to describe the sounds they hear using descriptive words to help expand their vocabularies.

Revisiting the Walk

Repeating a walk in the wind, either under the same windy conditions as the previous walk or under different conditions, allows children opportunities to expand their learning. It can be a time to revisit questions or test theories or it can simply be a time to repeat a fun experience with a wind toy.

Books

Asch, Frank, and Devin Asch. 2002. *Like a windy day*. San Diego: Harcourt.

Bauer, Marion Dane, and John Wallace. 2003. *Wind*. New York: Aladdin.

Burke, Jennifer S. 2000. *Windy days*. New York: Children's Press.

Dorros, Arthur. 1990. *Feel the wind*. New York: Harper & Row.

Ets, Marie Hall. 1963. *Gilberto and the wind*. New York: Viking Press.

Hill, Eric. 2000. *Spot's windy day and other stories*. New York: Grosset & Dunlap.

Hutchins, Pat. 2003. *The wind blew*. Lancaster, PA: Childcraft Education Corp.

Karas, G. Brian. 1998. *The windy day*. New York: Simon & Schuster Books for Young Readers.

McKee, David. 1998. *Elmer takes off*. New York: Lothrop, Lee & Shepard.

Milbourne, Anna, and Elena Temporin. 2007. *The windy day*. London: Usborne.

Mitra, Annie. 1998. *Chloe's windy day*. London: Levinson.

Root, Phyllis, and Helen Craig. 1997. *One windy Wednesday*. Cambridge, MA: Candlewick Press.

Schaefer, Lola M. 2000. *A windy day*. Mankato, MN: Pebble Books.

Slater, Teddy, Bill Langley, and Diana Wakeman. 1993. *Walt Disney's Winnie the Pooh and the blustery day*. New York: Disney Press.

Zolotow, Charlotte, and Stefano Vitale. 1995. *When the wind stops*. New York: HarperCollins.

Snowy Day Walk

Before the Walk

Most young children delight in playing in the snow and enjoy describing their experiences to others. Before the walk, invite the children to share their experiences with snow. What kinds of snow activities have they participated in? What types of clothing did they wear? Make a list on chart paper of the things children suggest and save the list of words to add to an existing word wall or weather-related word wall.

If you live in an area of the country where it does not snow, there are still opportunities to discuss snow and weather in general, such as by reading a variety of children's books about snow and bringing in examples of some of the clothing children might wear on a snowy day. Ask the children why they think it doesn't snow where they live, then discuss the weather conditions needed to produce snow. Invite children to imagine what a snowy day might be like and to create paintings or write short stories about an imagined snowy day.

A walk on a snowy day allows children an opportunity to

- notice the effect of snow
- learn about snowflakes
- observe how animals respond to snow
- consider the importance of snow

Words to Use and Learn

blizzard	powder	snowbank	snowman
blowing	sled/sledding	snowblower	snowplow
cold	slush	snowdrift	snowstorm
fluffy	snow	snowfall	snowsuit
frost	snowballs	snowflake	white

Things to Bring on the Walk

✓ a spiral notebook that includes the children's questions and notes about experiences that might interest them (provocations), and for noting your observations of the children during the walk

✓ writing and drawing tools

✓ backpacks or paper bags for collecting things

✓ clipboards with white paper for drawing and black paper for "catching" snowflakes

✓ a camera

✓ a tape recorder or other recording device

During the Walk

Some of the experiences you engage in with the children may depend on the type of day, specifically whether it is snowing or not. The atmosphere when it is snowing is quite different from the atmosphere when it is not snowing.

As you take children walking on either type of day, encourage them to be aware of their surroundings and to use their senses of sight, hearing, and touch to explore.

⟳ Using the Sense of Hearing

Ask the children to listen for sounds related to the snowy day. Do they hear snowplows or snowblowers? Do they hear people shoveling their walks or driveways? Do tires from vehicles make a crunching sound as they move across the snow? What other sounds do the children hear that indicate there is snow? Are clumps of snow falling from the trees? Are sounds "crisper" when there is snow on the ground? Alternatively, does sound appear muffled or hushed? Sometimes when it snows it becomes quiet and all you can hear are the sounds of the snow falling. Keep a list of all the sounds children hear related to snow and revisit the list when you are back inside. If you brought along a tape recorder, be sure to record the different sounds.

👁 Using the Sense of Sight

What does the sky look like when it snows? Can the children see the sky? Mention that when you can't see into the sky or when you can't see very far in front of you, it's called a "whiteout." If it's not snowing, what color is the sky? Is it dark? Does it look like it might snow soon? Is it too bright to look directly at the snow?

Look for things covered in snow. Can the children guess the object beneath the snow using its snow-covered shape as a clue? How does the snow change the appearance of things? For example, what do cars look like covered in snow? What do bushes or small trees look like covered in snow? Does anything blend in with the snow, making it harder to see?

What do the snowflakes look like? Are they large and fluffy or small and wet? Try to capture some snowflakes on your hand or mitten to examine before they melt. Can the children see how intricate and delicate they are? What kinds of designs or shapes make up a snowflake? Discuss with the children that no two snowflakes are alike, and encourage them to compare

👁 Using the Sense of Sight (Continued)

snowflakes when they land on their mittens or gloves.

Look for footprints and animal tracks in the snow. What footprints or tracks do the children see? Can they tell who made the footprints? Were they made by an adult or a child? What about the animal tracks? What kind of animal made the tracks? Look for vehicle tracks in the snow. What tracks do the children see? Can they tell the type of vehicle that made the tracks? How do they know?

Is anyone exercising in the snow, such as cross-country skiers?

Be sure to take plenty of photographs during the walk.

👄 Using the Sense of Taste

Have children try to catch snowflakes on their tongues. What does snow taste like? Does snow taste different from rain?

Using the Sense of Touch

If the children are interested, invite them to remove one of their mittens or gloves and feel the snow. How would they describe the snow? Is it heavy and slushy? Is it light and airy? Is the snow good for packing to make snowballs or snow forts? What kind of snow makes for the best sledding or skiing? Why?

Animals in the Snow

Talk about animals who live in climates where there is a lot of snow, such as rabbits, fox, and bears, and how the white color of their fur helps them hide from other animals. Do the children see any holes in the snow that might be an animal's hole or small den? Where do animals go when it snows? How do they find food?

Fun in the Snow

What kinds of things do people do for fun in the snow? Have the children ever built a snowman? Have the children ever built a snow fort? What is a snow fort? Have they ever made snow angels or had a snowball fight? Have they ever gone sledding? Encourage the children to share their experiences playing in the snow.

Playing Fox and Geese

Play this game in a large, open area of new snow. It is more fun to play with four or more players.

Stomp a big circle in the snow. Add two intersecting paths through the middle of the circle. Where the paths meet, stomp out a small "safe zone." The figure should look like a circle with an X in it, with a stomped-out circle in the center.

Choose one child to be the fox or you can be the fox at first. All other children are the geese. The fox chases the geese and tries to tag one of them. All children must run only on the paths, and geese can't be tagged when they are standing in the safe zone. When the fox tags a goose, that goose becomes the next fox.

 **After the Walk**

There are many ways to document the children's learning after a snow-day walk. Both older and younger children can be encouraged to create artwork in different mediums and techniques that depict entire snow-covered scenes or that focus on smaller details such as snowflakes. Consider reading the book *The Snowy Day* by Ezra Jack Keats to introduce children to Keats's mixed-media collage techniques.

Children may also be interested in helping create a life-size snow scene using real items from nature, such as tree branches and cotton batting. Ask children how they might create some of the things they observed outdoors, such as a snowman and walkways piled with snow. This display could become a permanent part of the room, with children helping to change the display with each new season.

Add cotton balls or cotton batting to the block area to encourage children to create structures covered in "snow." Add boxes children can cover in the cotton to create a ski resort.

Older Children

Discuss snow with the children to discover what about snow is most interesting to them. Some children might approach the topic from a more scientific perspective, such as the weather conditions needed to make snow. Invite them to research how snow is created naturally as well as how snow machines at ski hills create snow. Who invented the snow machine? Other children may be more interested in using materials, such as thin wire and tissue paper, to create snowflakes that could be hung from the ceiling or in front of windows.

People who live where it is snowy and cold for much of the year have many words to describe the snow. Invite the children to discover all of the different words people who live in these types of climates have for describing snow.

Have the children make a list of all the *snow* words they can think of, such as snowball, snowstorm, and snowflake. Then challenge them to write stories that incorporate all of the words they listed.

How would the children describe snow to a child who had never experienced it before? Have children create demonstrations involving the five senses to help describe the concept of snow. Encourage them to use props such as ice or snow-related clothing in their demonstrations.

Why do children like snow? What is it about snow that is so appealing to so many children? At what age does the fascination with snow begin to diminish—or does it ever diminish? Invite children to create short pieces of writing that help explain their fascination with snow.

Younger Children
Ask younger children to describe their experiences with the snow using their different senses. What does snow look like? What does snow sound like? What does snow feel like? What does snow taste like? What does snow smell like? While the children talk about snow, ask them open-ended questions to extend their learning and help them expand their vocabularies. Take note of the things children seem most excited about and consider ways they could demonstrate their learning. Would they enjoy setting up a life-size snow scene inside? Are they interested in how snow is created? Would they enjoy using sponge pieces dipped in white paint to dab over a scene to depict falling snow?

Create a class poem or a class story about snow. On a sheet of chart paper, record all of the things children share about snow. Consider prompting children with lines such as "My favorite thing about snow is . . ." or "If I were a snowflake, I would . . ."

Add snow-related words to an existing word wall or create a new word wall dedicated to snow-related words.

Help the children create snowflake stick puppets by cutting out construction paper in different shapes and gluing them to craft sticks. Remind children that no two snowflakes are alike. After they have created the snowflake puppets, invite them to put on a puppet show involving all of the different snowflake characters.

Print photographs taken during the walk. Invite the children to use the photographs to help create a class book titled "Our Snowy Day."

Revisiting the Walk

Chances are you will not need to convince the children to return to the snow another day. Try to choose a snowy day that is different from that of the previous walk to focus on similarities and differences between the two walks. Do children hear the same snow-related sounds or is it quieter? Why might that be? How is the snow different or the same?

Books

Bauer, Marion Dane, and John Wallace. 2003. *Snow*. New York: Aladdin.

Branley, Franklyn Mansfield, and Holly Keller. 1999. *Snow is falling*. New York: HarperCollins Publishers.

Briggs, Raymond. 1978. *The snowman*. New York: Random House.

Ehlert, Lois. 1999. *Snowballs*. San Diego: Harcourt Brace.

Flanagan, Alice K. 2003. *Snow*. Chanhassen, MN: Child's World.

Kaner, Etta, and Marie Lafrance. 2006. *Who likes snow?* Toronto: Kids Can Press.

Keats, Ezra Jack. 2005. *The snowy day*. New York: Viking Press.

Marsico, Katie. 2007. *Snowy weather days*. New York: Children's Press.

Mayer, Mercer. 2006. *Just a snowy day*. New York: HarperFestival.

Prelutsky, Jack, and Yossi Abolafia. 2006. *It's snowing! It's snowing! Winter poems*. New York: HarperCollins.

Rustad, Martha E. H. 2006. *How's the weather? Today is snowy*. Mankato, MN: Capstone Press.

Rylant, Cynthia, and Lauren Stringer. 2008. *Snow*. Orlando: Harcourt.

Sherman, Josepha, and Jeff Yesh. 2004. *Flakes and flurries: A book about snow*. Minneapolis: Picture Window Books.

Shulevitz, Uri. 1998. *Snow*. New York: Farrar Straus Giroux.

Yee, Wong Herbert. 2003. *Tracks in the snow*. New York: H. Holt.

Animals and Birds Walk

Before the Walk

Most children are curious about small animals and birds, their comings and goings. Taking children on a walk to observe these living creatures will be an exciting adventure and can help children learn more about small animals and birds. On these excursions, children can also

- observe an animal's characteristics and how it behaves
- see where an animal lives
- watch how animals eat and gather food
- notice whether an animal stays by itself or is found in a group
- learn how animals approach others and what their favorite activities might be
- look for clues of an animal's presence

Prior to walking with the children, discuss with them their experiences with animals and birds, including pets they may have at home. Encourage children to tell about where their pets stay, what they eat, and whether their pets go outside. Introduce the idea of domestic, or tame, animals. What makes an animal or bird tame? Then talk about wild animals that might be found outside. What makes an animal or bird wild?

Wonder what wild animals and birds eat, what they do during the day, and where they sleep. Make a list with the children of all the animals and birds—tame and wild—they might see on a walk.

Use magazines or books to find pictures of birds and animals. Older children in particular may be interested in books containing realistic drawings of animals and birds, such as Audubon sketches. Encourage children to notice some of the identifying characteristics of animals and birds. Talk about the types of birds or small animals you might find this time of year. Plan to look for animals at another time of the year as well.

Younger children in particular might enjoy making binoculars to use to "spy" animals or birds during the walk. To make binoculars, collect empty toilet-paper rolls, two for each child. The rolls can be colored or covered with contact paper. Then staple together two toilet-paper rolls. Create a carrying strap so that children can wear the tubes like binoculars. Punch a hole in the outside edges of each tube and thread yarn or ribbon through them. Tie the ends of the thread or ribbon together, allowing enough length to go around a child's neck to hang like binoculars. *Watch children carefully whenever they wear the binoculars around their necks to prevent the possibility of strangulation.*

Words to Use and Learn

animal	feather	nest	tail
beak	fur	paw	tame
bird	hair	pet	whisker
cat	legs	rabbit	wild
dog	mammal	squirrel	wing

Things to Bring on the Walk

✓ a spiral notebook that includes the children's questions and notes about experiences that might interest them (provocations), and for noting your observations of the children during the walk

✓ a camera

✓ clipboards and paper for the children

✓ writing and drawing tools

✓ homemade binoculars

✓ bread crumbs or stale sliced bread

✓ small bags of birdseed

✓ small-animal and bird guides

✓ backpacks or paper bags for collecting things

✓ a tape recorder or other device for recording animal and bird sounds

During the Walk

Use the ideas generated from prior discussions with the children about animals and birds to guide your explorations during the walk. The following activities may also be helpful.

👁 Using the Sense of Sight

Invite children to look for animals. List the animals they identify. Are the animals tame or wild? How do the children know? Are the animals on a leash, in a fenced area, or tied up? Are the animals running free? What are the animals doing? Notice the physical characteristics of the animals, including their colors and sizes. Decide whether any of them are still young (puppies or kittens, for example). Notice the different ways the animals move and behave.

Encourage older children to create lists of the animals and birds they see. Then try to identify them as members of a specific category, such as birds, but also as a specific kind of bird, such as a robin. Children can look through the guide books to help them in the identification process.

Have younger children put on their binoculars and look for birds. Share with children that some people spend a lot of time looking for birds, or bird watching. Bird watchers usually wear binoculars to help them spot birds more easily. Watch at bird feeders to see whether many birds come and go. If there are trees near the feeders, are there birds in them?

Look for signs of animal life even when you can't see the animals. Look for doghouses or pens, holes in trees, molehills, or birds' nests. Look for footprints and tracks in the mud or snow. Look for wet footprints on the sidewalk or pavement.

🦻 Using the Sense of Hearing

Listen for the sounds of animals and birds. Have the children close their eyes and listen. Can they tell what animals or birds might be around from the sounds they hear?

Listen for sounds other than vocalizations associated with animal life, such as rustling of bushes or trees, pecking on wood, or flapping of wings.

Record the different sounds you hear so children can listen to them again after the walk.

Using the Sense of Touch

If you're near a pet animal, bird, or reptile that can be touched, encourage children to feel the different textures of body coverings. Talk about what makes an animal or bird feel the ways it does. How does a cat's fur feel different from a bird's feathers or a lizard's skin?

Wondering about Animals and Birds

Have children think about where different wild creatures live at different times of the year. What do they do in the wintertime? Do they need shelter all the time or just when they have babies? Wonder if they live in families or groups of their own. How do they feed their babies?

Think about the foods the creatures eat and wonder how they find their food. Do they have trouble finding food at some times of the year, and what do they do about it? Can we help?

How do creatures protect themselves from each other? Do they fight or bother each other? Observing animals and birds at different seasons of the year will help children gather more information to help them answer these questions.

Drawing and Writing about Animals and Birds

For children who enjoy drawing, encourage them to draw pictures of animals and birds, pets as well as wild creatures. Or children can jot down "field notes," including questions they may have about the creatures they observed.

Photographing Animals and Birds

Use a camera to take pictures of the birds and animals seen during the walk. Back inside, children can refer to the photographs to help them document their learning. The photos can also be used to create class books.

Some Safety Notes

During the walk, there may be opportunities to pet or touch neighborhood pets, but use caution in approaching unknown animals. Allow children who are frightened of animals to remain at a safe distance. Encourage children to watch the animal or bird, but don't force any close encounters. Never pet unknown animals, because animals of any size can present a hazard. If a neighbor or person walking a dog says it's okay to pet an animal and that the pet is child friendly, it's usually all right to do so. Never approach a dog when it's growling. Use encounters with small animals to teach the children how to safely approach animals.

 **After the Walk**

Discuss with the children highlights from the walk or things they found most interesting about the animals and birds they observed. Are the children able to make some generalizations about the creatures they observed nearby? For example, are all dogs on leashes? Are all birds in the area called pigeons?

Be sure to share photos taken of the animals and birds observed during the walk. They can help refresh the children's memories and be used to help the children think of ways to document their learning about animals and birds.

Older Children

School-age children are likely to have a number of ideas related to the various animals and birds they observed during the walk. Ask open-ended questions to help them expand their learning and discover ways of sharing their learning with others. If children need help thinking of what to do, suggest one or two of the following ideas.

Create board games such as lotto games, matching games, and animal-category games. You can download directions for making these games from the Redleaf Web site, www.redleafpress.org. Enter "Hey Kids!" into the search field and follow the links.

Create dioramas, or mini landscapes, showing animals and birds in their natural habitats.

Use playdough, clay, wire, or foil to create sculptures of animals or birds.

Paint a mural that includes all of the creatures children observed during the walk.

Use the photographs to create collages.

Encourage children who drew sketches of animals and birds or who took field notes to use their drawings and notes to create their own guide books.

Explain what fables are and share some examples of fables that include animals who speak. Encourage children to create their own fables using animals they observed during the walk.

Create animal and bird finger puppets or lunch-bag puppets. Children can use their puppets to create their own puppet shows or dramatize fables they may have written.

Explain haiku poems and invite children to create their own haikus about the creatures they observed. Haiku poems consist of three lines that do not rhyme: the first line contains five syllables, the second line contains seven syllables, and the third line contains five syllables. Make sure children understand that syllables are the breaks in a word. For example, *bird* has one syllable; *rabbit* has two syllables; *animal* has three syllables; and *dictionary* has four syllables. Read some examples of haiku poetry to the children if needed.

Younger Children

Toddlers and preschool-age children learn best through sensory exploration and movement. Consider replaying recordings you made of animal sounds or other sounds related to animals. Have children guess which animals made the particular sounds. Then work with the children to create their own animal sounds.

Place a variety of fabric scraps in a feely box, such as fuzzy, furry, feathery, and smooth fabrics. Have the children describe the fabrics and the animals whose body coverings are most like the fabrics.

Create animal headbands to represent animals you saw on the walk, such as rabbit ears or frog eyes. Have the children wear the headbands and imitate the actions of the animals: rabbits hopping, frogs jumping, dogs running and barking.

Purchase or make animal and bird finger puppets. Children can use them to create their own puppet shows or recite familiar fingerplays.

Add new animal- and bird-related vocabulary to an existing word wall.

Display photographs or posters of animals and birds. Create simple labels on index cards of the creatures' names, such as dog, puppy, owl, and nest, and tape them near the photographs or posters.

Use the photos to create an illustrated dictionary of animals and birds that the children can use.

Revisiting the Walk

Take several walks during the year to observe the different behaviors of animals and birds. Can all of the creatures observed earlier still be seen?

Where did they go? Do they look the same? How have they changed?

Books

Aloian, Molly, and Bobbie Kalman. 2005. *Many kinds of animals.* New York: Crabtree.

Armentrout, David, and Patricia Armentrout. 2003. *Animals.* Vero Beach, FL: Rourke Publishing.

Arnosky, Jim. 1993. *Crinkleroot's 25 birds every child should know.* New York: Bradbury Press.

Backstein, Karen, and Henri Galeron. 2003. *Cats.* New York: Scholastic.

Bailey, Jill, and David Burnie. 1992. *Birds.* New York: Dorling Kindersley.

Boring, Mel, and Linda Garrow. 2000. *Rabbits, squirrels, and chipmunks.* Young naturalist field guides. Milwaukee, WI: Gareth Stevens.

Carter, David A. 2007. *Whoo? Whoo?* New York: Little Simon.

———. 2008. *Woof! Woof!* New York: Little Simon.

Deschamps, Nicola. 2001. *Pets.* London: Dorling Kindersley.

Ehlert, Lois. 2008. *Oodles of animals.* Orlando: Harcourt.

Flack, Marjorie. 1997. *Angus and the cat.* New York: Farrar, Straus & Giroux.

Fox, Olga, Mark Fox, and Andrea Blake. 2001. *Discovering birds.* Ballarat, VIC: Wizard Books.

Gibbons, Gail. 2001. *Ducks.* New York: Holiday House.

Kalman, Bobbie, and Kathryn Smithyman. 2002. *The life cycle of a bird.* New York: Crabtree.

Williams, Sue, and Julie Vivas. 1998. *I went walking.* Orlando: Harcourt Brace.

Insects and Spiders Walk

Before the Walk

Many parents and child care providers alike have experienced a young child arriving at home or school with some kind of bug in hand. Most children—although not all—are fascinated with bugs and delight in holding ladybugs and caterpillars. Before taking a bug walk with the children, try to determine their attitudes about and knowledge of insects and spiders. What aspects of the tiny creatures fascinate them most? Let their interests guide your explorations of bugs during the walk. Read several books about bugs to younger children prior to the walk.

A bug walk provides children with opportunities to

- consider different types of bugs, including the difference between insects and spiders
- notice the characteristics of insects, spiders, and other small creatures
- observe how bugs work and behave
- learn where bugs live and about their life cycles
- become aware of insects and spiders to avoid
- find out how to collect and care for bugs without squishing them

Because there are so many different types of bugs, plan several walks to observe them under different conditions. Consider spreading your bug watching throughout the year. Some insects, such as bees, are busy working in the spring, but are more troublesome in August or September. Spiders may be more plentiful in dry weather and in early fall.

Children of all ages may enjoy bringing along containers for collecting insects. You can download instructions for making bug boxes from the Redleaf Web site, www.redleafpress.org. Enter "Hey Kids!" into the search field and follow the links.

Words to Use and Learn

ant	caterpillar	firefly	ladybug
antennae	chrysalis	fly	mosquito
anthill	cocoon	grasshopper	spider
bee	colony	hive	spiderweb
butterfly	cricket	insect	worm

Things to Bring on the Walk

✓ a spiral notebook that includes the children's questions and notes about experiences that might interest them (provocations), and for noting your observations of the children during the walk

✓ a camera

✓ clipboards and paper for the children

✓ writing and drawing tools

✓ bug boxes

✓ magnifying glasses

✓ trowels

✓ a tape recorder or other device for recording sounds

✓ bug nets

During the Walk

Consider using some of the following suggestions during the walk to help children learn about bugs. Should children discover other aspects of bugs that interest them, be sure to help them pursue and later document those interests.

👁 Using the Sense of Sight

Keep an eye out for insects and spiders. Notice which settings may have more bugs in them and what types of bugs live there. Under eaves may be good places to find spiderwebs and spiders, trees and shrubs may have caterpillars and beetles, and flowers attract bees. Search grassy areas for anthills. Is there a trail of ants? Also search under rocks, on tree bark, and on leaves of plants, and use trowels to search in the soil for various types of insects.

Put out some food, such as raisins or crackers, to attract insects. Watch how insects move and how they eat or try out food.

Use the magnifying glasses to look on leaves for white or pale-colored eggs or other stages in the insects' life cycles. Abandoned wasps' nests, honeycombs, or cocoons are particularly interesting if found, and can be used to discuss many things related to insects, such as life cycles, homes, and things (such as honey) created by insects.

 ### Using the Sense of Touch

Talk about how it feels to hold an insect or have one crawling on you. Some children may not like the idea and shouldn't be required to hold insects if resistant.

Notice the differences in how insects, caterpillars, and worms feel. Some are smooth, others are rough or furry.

Identifying Bugs

Use the magnifying glasses to help identify insects and spiders. Count legs to help in the identifying process. All insects have six legs, so even though a creature looks like an insect, if it has more than six legs, such as a spider, it isn't an insect.

Point out the insect's antennae, or feelers, which grow out of the head or front part of an insect. Most insects have three pairs of legs, one pair of antennae, and one or two pairs of wings. See how many body parts you and the children can identify. It's easiest to identify parts on ants or ladybugs, which you can hold in your hand, and occasionally on large flies, which may pause on an arm or speck of food. Other identifying characteristics are wings, coloring, and size and shape of body.

If you discover worms on the walk, discuss with the children whether worms are insects or not. If not, what type of creature are worms?

Wondering about Bugs

Ask the children what happens to bugs at different times of the year. Do they go underground, hide in trees, or die when it gets cold? How long do bugs usually live?

How do new bug cities get started? How do the worker insects know what to do when they live in colonies? How can ants carry such heavy loads?

Do insects fight with each other? How do they protect themselves from predators?

Look at insects at different times of the year to answer these questions or other questions children might ask. Consider collecting different insects in the bug boxes to observe changes over a period of time. Collect caterpillars to watch their life cycle.

Drawing Bugs

Some children may enjoy drawing pictures of bugs in their natural habitats, such as ants going to and from an anthill or bees landing on flowers. Children can also refer to their drawings as guides for creating bug habitats after the walk.

Photographing Bugs

Be sure to take photographs of the children exploring bugs as well as close-ups of the bugs themselves.

After the Walk

Did the children collect any live bugs from the walk? If so, discuss ways of setting up displays of the bugs in jars or habitats (see the book list for suggestions). Work with the children to establish an enticing and visually pleasing display area for the bugs inside. Remember, do not "borrow" a creature for too long—gently return bugs to the place they were found within a day or two, if not sooner.

Share the digital photos with the children or make copies of photographs as soon as possible.

Older Children
What kinds of things did the older children in your group collect during the bug walk? Did they collect live bugs, and if so, how do they plan to keep them alive inside?

The life cycles of bugs can be a fascinating topic for older children. Did the children collect insect eggs or cocoons—any items that could be used to create a three-dimensional display of an insect's life cycle?

Perhaps a child is interested in the important environmental work of bugs. What kinds of work do different insects and spiders perform? There are several books in the book list children could use to further their study of the work of insects and spiders.

Have children select a favorite insect or spider and make a book about its life cycle, complete with illustrations. Children may need to do some

research first. Invite children to share their books with others when they are complete.

Create a bug dictionary. How many words can children think of related to bugs? Also consider additional meanings of words such as *bug*. In the sentence "You bug me," what does *bug* mean?

Create insect and spider puppets from paper lunch bags. Children can then use their puppets to create a play about bugs for the younger children.

Invite children to create books called "A Day in the Life of a(n) [insect or spider of their choice]." Children might choose to do research beforehand to determine how long certain insects or spiders live. Do any insects or spiders live only for one day? What might that bug do with his or her "one day"?

Younger Children
Perhaps you noticed during the walk the ways different children chose to explore bugs. To get them thinking about ways to document their learning, it may be helpful to share some of the photographs showing them engaged in specific activities. Did they enjoy holding bugs and examining their different body parts? If so, perhaps they would enjoy creating models of bugs using clay, toothpicks, and wire.

Invite the children to think about a specific body part of an insect or spider, such as the very fine wings on insects. Which materials might the children use to create insect wings? Consider making materials available—such as different-colored, transparent papers—for the children to use to create wings. A study of wings might then lead to an interest in flight and other creatures that fly. How are the wings of insects different from the wings of birds? What about creating a "wing display" that demonstrates a child's learning about and understanding of different creatures' wings?

Purchase or make bug finger puppets. Children can use them to recite familiar fingerplays or ones of their own.

Make a class book called "Bug Homes." Children can draw pictures of or write about bug homes they observed during the walk.

Add new bug-related vocabulary to an existing word wall.

Make a list on chart paper of all the bugs the children observed during the walk. Draw simple illustrations next to each bug's name. Then, on a new sheet of chart paper, create a short rebus story incorporating some of the bugs from the list. Invite children to help you read the rebus story by saying the name of the bug when they see its picture in the story.

 **Revisiting the Walk**

Take several insects and spiders walks throughout the year to follow up on the bugs observed during the initial walk. Are the bugs still visible? What kinds of activities are they performing now? Perhaps the bugs have disappeared altogether. Where did they go?

Books

Clarke, Ginjer L., and Pete Mueller. 2007. *Bug out! The world's creepiest, crawliest critters.* New York: Grosset & Dunlap.

Crowley, Ned. 2006. *Ugh! A bug!* Minneapolis: Millbrook Press.

DeGezelle, Terri. 2000. *Bugs A to Z.* Mankato, MN: Capstone Curriculum.

Fleming, Denise. 2007. *Beetle bop.* New York: Harcourt.

Holmes, Anita. 2001. *Insect detector.* New York: Benchmark Books.

Horacek, Petr. 2007. *Butterfly, butterfly.* Cambridge, MA: Candlewick Press.

Jeunesse, Gallimard, Sylvaine Peyrols, Christina Cramer, and Louise Goldsen. 2003. *Ladybugs and other insects.* New York: Scholastic Reference.

Kalman, Bobbie. 2004. *Life cycle of an earthworm.* New York: Crabtree.

————. 2004. *Life cycle of a mosquito.* New York: Crabtree.

Lackner, Michelle Myers, and Daniel Powers. 2001. *Toil in the soil.* Brookfield, CT: Millbrook Press.

Loewen, Nancy, and Rick Peterson. 2006. *Garden wigglers: Earthworms in your backyard.* Minneapolis: Picture Window Books.

Parker, Steve, and Richard Draper. 2007. *I love bugs.* New York: Back Pack Books.

Schulte, Mary. 2005. Ants and other insects. New York: Children's Press.

Sill, Cathryn P., and John Sill. 2000. *About insects: A guide for children.* Atlanta: Peachtree.

York, Penelope. 2002. *Bugs.* New York: Dorling Kindersley.

Trees Walk

Before the Walk

Children benefit in many ways when they are exposed to and become connected with the natural world. This fact, coupled with today's emphasis on "going green," makes it more important than ever to integrate nature into children's daily lives and educational experiences.

The best way for children to learn about trees and why they are important is to observe and study them in their own yards, neighborhoods, or school settings. A tree walk can help children

- observe seasonal changes and the yearly cycle and growth of trees

- learn the names of different types of trees, and some specific trees

- notice the various parts of trees, their characteristics, and differences among trees

- consider what trees provide for people and animals

- look at the many uses people make of tree products

- appreciate the beauty of trees

To get children thinking about trees, create a tree display that includes leaves, bark, acorns, nuts, berries, and pine needles along with magnifying glasses. Also include products made from trees, such as paper, pencils, small pieces of lumber, and a bottle of maple syrup. If possible, include a cross section of a tree to show how to determine a tree's age by the number of rings in the cross section. Include photographs of trees, field guides, or catalogs from local nurseries. Allow children to examine the items and use them to stimulate discussions. Ask the children if the trees in the photos or books look the same as the trees around where they live. Why or why not?

Add books about trees and nature to library and literacy areas on a regular basis, and look at them as revisits take place, adding new perspectives and expanding children's thinking each time.

Words to Use and Learn

acorn	forest	pine	shade
bark	leaf	pinecones	tree
berries	needles	roots	trunk
crown	nuts	sapling	twig
evergreen	oak	seeds	wood

Things to Bring on the Walk

✓ a spiral notebook that includes the children's questions and notes about experiences that might interest them (provocations), and for noting your observations of the children during the walk

✓ measuring tools, such as tape measures, rulers, or string

✓ backpacks or paper bags for collecting things

✓ tape

✓ paper, pencils, pens, crayons

✓ a camera

✓ a tape recorder or other recording device

✓ pictures of trees or field guides to trees

During the Walk

Use the ideas generated from prior discussions with the children about trees to guide your explorations during the walk. The following activities may also be helpful.

Identifying Trees

Use the photographs or field guides to help children identify the trees they see. Talk about the parts of trees that help identify them, such as size, bark, leaves or needles, pinecones, nuts, or berries. Keep a list of the trees you identify, and encourage older children to keep their own lists. Also consider taping a leaf or other feature of the tree next to its name as a tree is identified. If a tree cannot be identified, collect a leaf or bark sample so you and the children can look it up later.

Collecting Items from Trees

Children can use bags to collect nuts, seeds, pinecones, and leaves to use for later documentation projects. You might want to collect and label some master samples so you'll be able to help sort out and identify items in the children's collections later on.

Observing Trees

Notice the shade around trees. Decide which trees would be good for climbing and which would be good for sitting under. Look for unusual things about the trees: split trunks or branches, strange formations, or trees that bend in one direction. Wonder what caused these things.

Look for signs of animal life around trees. Are there birds, squirrels, or insects using the trees? Watch quietly for any signs of life in the trees.

Are there birds' nests or squirrels' nests? Listen for sounds of birds singing or pecking at trees or squirrels running up and down trees.

Take photographs of the trees. Encourage children to draw pictures of the trees as well.

Wondering about Trees

Look for things that are edible from trees and things that are nonedible (or even poisonous). What things do animals or birds eat from trees?

Notice the trunks of large trees and the heavy root structure going into the ground. Guess how far the roots of the tree may go and make a circle around the tree to show how far the roots may extend. Can you see any roots for the small trees? The root systems go under the ground and spread out to take up as much room under the ground as the branches and leaves (the crown of the tree) take up above the ground. Measure the distance from the base of the tree trunk to the base of the crown. Talk about what the roots do for the tree. Do the roots of trees ever cause problems? What kinds? Make some guesses about roots of big and little trees. Why are some very small trees supported by stakes and ropes?

Comparing Trees

Stop and carefully examine several different trees. Look at size, shape, color, and texture. Notice the trunk, bark, and leaf structure and name those parts of the tree. Talk about the differences in the trees. Call the children's attention to the difference between evergreen trees and deciduous trees in terms of structure, texture, and color. Pick a favorite example of each kind of tree. Plan to visit the trees frequently during the year to watch what happens to them (such as bearing fruit, shedding leaves, and new growth).

Take a tape measure and measure around the trunks. Children can also measure with their arms; some very large trees will need two or more children to reach around them.

 Using the Senses

Have the children examine the trees in multisensory ways. Huddle up close to the trunk of the tree and look up at the sky through the branches. Feel the textures of the trees, their leaves and bark. Children can use crayons and paper to make rubbings of the bark.

Invite children to close their eyes and listen to the trees. Can they hear them? What can the children tell about them? Look at trees from a distance as well, to take in the whole effect.

Talking about Trees

Encourage the children to describe how the trees look to them and the things about the trees that especially interest them. As the year progresses, ask the children the same questions about the same trees. Do they still feel the same way about the same trees? Why or why not? What about the trees has changed? Talk about what happens to the trees during each season.

Make some generalizations about some of the trees you have seen related to size, branch structure, and so on. Here are some examples: Evergreen trees have branches that start right at the ground while other trees have branches high up, off the ground. New trees have very small trunks; older trees have thick trunks. Write these things in your notebook or encourage older children to record them. These observations could be useful when children begin considering ways to document their learning about trees after the walk.

After the Walk

Talk with the children about the trees they observed and the items they may have collected during the walk. Children will likely want to discuss many things and continue to learn about trees. Be sure to share with the children the photographs taken of trees during the walk.

Older Children

School-age children can demonstrate their learning about trees in a variety of ways according to their interests. For example, they could create a seasonal mural showing how trees and their foliage look during each season. Items collected from the walks, such as leaves, pinecones, and berries, can be glued to the mural to show how the trees change with the seasons. This mural creates opportunities for reinforcing vocabulary such as *deciduous* and *coniferous*.

For children interested in ecology and tree conservation, work with them to research local or national groups dedicated to preserving trees and forests. What opportunities are there for all of the children to become involved in local volunteer activities, such as planting trees?

Children can use items collected to create their own tree guides by gluing items to the pages of their books. They can include information about different species from other books as well as things they discovered on their own during the walks.

Invite children to create "Me Trees." Me Trees are similar to Family Trees, but document children's own experiences and milestones, beginning with their birth on lower branches. The highest branches represent their most recent experiences and milestones.

Trees evoke different emotions in different people, and as such have been the subject of many poems throughout the ages. Collect a variety of poems about trees and share them with the children. Discuss with children the different emotions trees evoke, and why. Then invite children to create their own poems about trees using descriptive words that evoke some of their own feelings about trees.

If trees could talk, what would they say? Invite children to create a drama or public service message involving talking trees.

Younger Children

There are many ways young children can demonstrate and expand their learning about trees. They will delight in working with items collected during the walks as well as trying to replicate trees and the features of trees with craft materials.

Add new words related to trees to an existing word wall.

Create a class book about trees or have each child create his own book using items collected during the walk.

How many things in the room begin with the letter T as in tree? Search for things that begin with the letter T and make a list of the words you find. Then transfer the words to a sheet of chart paper.

Draw simple pictures next to the words so children can begin associating the things with their written names.

Each day for five days read children a different book about trees. At the end of the week, invite them to share which book was their favorite and why. Reread the books children enjoyed most.

 ## Revisiting the Walk

Try to observe the same trees throughout the year; think about taking this walk on a regular basis to observe changes. The children can learn about trees a little at a time, and you can extend the discussions and activities over a period of time. Children's interest in nature is ongoing, and trees easily lend themselves to review and revisiting. If the trees change, ask the children to describe the change. Invite children to re-create art they created after the first walk to reflect the change in the trees.

Books

Bernard, Robin. 2001. *A tree for all seasons.* Washington, DC: National Geographic Society.

Bourgoing, Pascale de, and Christian Broutin. 1992. *The tree.* New York: Cartwheel Books.

Cooper, Jason. 2003. *Oak tree.* Vero Beach, FL: Rourke Publishing.

Ehlert, Lois. 1991. *Red leaf, yellow leaf.* Orlando: Harcourt Brace.

Florian, Douglas. 1990. *Discovering trees.* New York: Aladdin Books.

Fowler, Allan. 1990. *It could still be a tree.* Chicago: Children's Press.

———. 2001. *Maple trees.* Chicago: Children's Press.

George, Kristine O'Connell, and Kate Kiesler. 1998. *Old Elm speaks: Tree poems.* New York: Clarion Books.

Gibbons, Gail. 2002. *Tell me, tree: All about trees for kids.* Boston: Little, Brown & Co.

Godwin, Sam, and Simone Abel. 2001. *From little acorns: A first look at the life cycle of a tree.* London: Hodder Wayland.

Maestro, Betsy, and Loretta Krupinski. 1994. *Why do leaves change color?* New York: HarperCollins.

Oppenheim, Joanne, Jean Tseng, and Mou-Sien Tseng. 1995. *Have you seen trees?* New York: Scholastic.

Pluckrose, Henry Arthur. 1994. *Trees.* Chicago: Children's Press.

Tagliaferro, Linda. 2007. *Life cycle of a pine tree.* Mankato, MN: Capstone Press.

Worth, Bonnie. 2006. *I can name 50 trees today!* New York: Random House.

Flowers and Plants Walk

Before the Walk

It may be best to take this walk during the spring and summer months, when most flowers and flowering shrubs are in full bloom. However, if there is a floral shop or nursery nearby, make the floral shop or nursery your destination and modify the activities in this walk accordingly.

To get younger children thinking about flowers and plants, bring in a few bouquets and place them around the room in jars or vases. See how long it takes the children to notice them. Then gather the flowers in one location and begin a discussion with the children to find out what they already know about flowers and plants. Ask older children whether they have had any experiences growing flowers or arranging them. Do any of the children have favorite flowers?

Preview the walk to discover the flowers or plants currently growing or in bloom in the area. Show the children pictures of the flowers or plants and invite the children to look for them during the walk. Research how plants grow and make their own

food (photosynthesis) so that you can explain the process to older children.

Walks that invite children to notice flowers and plants offer opportunities for children to

- learn the names of different types of flowers, including where and how they grow
- discuss different ways people use flowers
- think about how other creatures benefit from and help flowers and plants
- find out about seasonal changes and growth cycles
- appreciate and pay attention to details in nature, such as shapes, colors, and textures
- consider how flowers and plants enhance environments, both indoors and outdoors

Words to Use and Learn

bloom	leaf	root	stem
bulb	light	seed	sun
clipper	petal	shade	trellis
cutting	photosynthesis	soil	vine
garden	pollen	stalk	

the names of flowers and plants that are common to your area

Things to Bring on the Walk

✓ a spiral notebook that includes the children's questions and notes about experiences that might interest them (provocations), and for noting your observations of the children during the walk

✓ writing and drawing tools

✓ clipboards and paper for the children

✓ a camera

✓ backpacks or paper bags for collecting things

✓ measuring tools, such as tape measures, rulers, or string

✓ a clipper for cutting samples, if appropriate

✓ pictures of flowers and plants to look for

✓ a tape recorder or other recording device

During the Walk

Consider using some of the following suggestions to help children focus on plants and flowers during the walk. Should children discover other aspects of plants and flowers that interest them, be sure to help them pursue and later document those interests.

Observing and Speculating about Flowers and Plants

Have the children look for plants or flowers you discussed prior to the walk. Talk about some of the characteristics of the flowers and plants, such as color, shape and texture of petals or leaves, and size. Take photographs and have the children draw the flowers and plants.

How many different flowers do you see? How many different plants do you see? How are flowers and plants used near homes, parks, or businesses? Are they used in borders, window boxes, planters, pots, or gardens? How do they enhance the landscape of these buildings or environments?

Do some plants and flowers grow better in the direct sunlight and some grow better in the shade? Which grow better in the sun? Which grow better in the shade? Look for plants that will have berries later on, such as blueberry and raspberry bushes and strawberry plants.

Do any birds or animals eat the flowers or plants? Which creatures help plants and flowers grow?

How do bees help flowers and plants? How do ladybugs help flowers or plants? Which creatures are harmful to flowers and plants?

Have children keep a list of all the different colors of flowers and plants that they see. Do one or two colors stand out more than others? Which colors are they? Collect samples of leaves or petals, if appropriate, to help identify unknown plants later on.

Talk about how plants grow and what they need to grow. For younger children, explain how plants need sunshine and water to grow. For older children, discuss photosynthesis, or how plants make their own food by turning carbon dioxide and water into sugar and oxygen. Are there any bees flying around certain flowers or bushes? Are they landing on the flowers or plants? Discuss the important work of certain insects, such as bees, which help pollinate flowers and plants.

Measuring Flowers and Plants

Use the measuring tools to measure the height of different flowers and plants. Which are the tallest? Which are the shortest? How much taller might they grow? What happens when some plants get too tall? Are there any plants with stakes next to them to prevent them from toppling over? What are the lengths of different petals and leaves?

Using the Sense of Smell

Have the children get up close and smell certain flowers and plants, such as roses and herbs. Do some flowers smell better than others? Are some more fragrant?

Are the children familiar with the names of herbs? Do they have any herbs growing at home?

Some Safety Notes

Talk about plant safety, such as not touching plants you're not familiar with. Explain that some plants, such as poison ivy and poison oak, can cause rashes that are very uncomfortable and itchy.

Remind children that they should never put any plants or flowers in their mouths, as some plants, such as mushrooms, can make a person very sick.

 **After the Walk**

Discuss the types of plants and flowers children saw during the walk. Were there any plants and flowers you couldn't identify? If you brought back samples of leaves or petals, work with the children to try to identify them using flower and plant guides.

What did the children learn about flowers and plants that they didn't know before the walk? Did they observe anything special, such as bees pollinating flowers? Did they notice any ladybugs controlling pests on plants? Did they see any hummingbirds drinking nectar from plants or flowers?

Older Children

There are many creative ways children can demonstrate their learning about plants and flowers through a variety of art mediums. Encourage children to experiment with creating sculptures of the flowers from clay, isolating each petal by adding them to the flower one at a time.

Talk with the children about botanical drawings and show them examples from books. Children can create their own botanical studies of plants and flowers using pen and ink or watercolors.

Encourage children to keep nature journals in which they list their observations of plants and flowers, complete with detailed illustrations.

Ask children to consider why people give flowers as gifts. What emotions are evoked when giving or receiving flowers? Ask children to write about

these things in their nature journals and share them with the group when they are finished writing.

Have children create a dictionary listing the names of local plants and flowers. Encourage them to illustrate each entry with drawings or pictures from gardening magazines or catalogs.

Invite children to write haiku poems about flowers. Haiku poems consist of three lines that do not rhyme: the first line contains five syllables, the second line contains seven syllables, and the third line contains five syllables. Make sure children understand that syllables are the breaks in a word. For example, *plant* has one syllable; *flower* has two syllables; *gardening* has three syllables; and *geranium* has four syllables. Read some examples of haiku poetry to the children if needed.

Younger Children

Work with the children to create a flower shop in the dramatic play area. These are some items you might consider adding to the area: clothes, such as aprons and gardening gloves; a toy cash register with play money; silk and plastic flowers and plants; plain note cards for messages on bouquets or arrangements; baskets or plastic tubs; plastic vases; a toy phone; a desk and chair; ribbons or raffia; butcher paper; and markers. Talk with the children about what employees do in flower shops.

Invite children to paint pictures of flowers and plants, experimenting with bold and bright colors. Or have the children consider planting a garden near the center. Work with them to consider an area that would work for the garden and to decide what plants or flowers to grow.

Talk with the children about taking care of cut flowers. Share with them that they should not leave flowers out of water for long periods of time, that they shouldn't put flowers in warm places, such as on bright windowsills, and that they should follow the directions on flower-food packages when placing flowers in vases or containers. Children can create signs with this information to display in the flower shop in the dramatic play center.

Add plant- and flower-related words to an existing word wall or create a new word wall dedicated to

plants and flowers near the flower shop in the room.

Gather books about flowers and plants from your local library or bookseller. Read at least one book each day to the children.

Invite the children to create flower puppets from craft sticks showing the life cycle of plants or flowers as well as the things they need to grow, such as water, sunshine, and insects, such as bees. Children can create a puppet show using the different craft-stick puppets in any way they desire.

 ## Revisiting the Walk

Return to the same areas where you observed flowers and plants during different times of the year. What happened to the flowers and plants?

Will they come back again in the spring or summer? Be sure to note when you start seeing signs of their return.

Books

Aston, Dianna Hutts, and Sylvia Long. 2007. *A seed is sleepy.* San Francisco: Chronicle Books.

Bunting, Eve, and Kathryn Hewitt. 1994. *Flower garden.* San Diego: Harcourt Brace Jovanovich.

———. 1996. *Sunflower house.* San Diego: Harcourt Brace.

Carle, Eric. 2001. *The tiny seed.* New York: Aladdin Paperbacks.

Cole, Henry. 1997. *Jack's garden.* New York: Mulberry Books.

Eclare, Melanie. 2000. *A handful of sunshine.* Brooklyn, NY: Ragged Bears.

Ehlert, Lois. 1988. *Planting a rainbow.* San Diego: Harcourt Brace Jovanovich.

Gibbons, Gail. 1991. *From seed to plant.* New York: Holiday House.

Hall, Zoe, and Shari Halpern. 1998. *The surprise garden.* New York: Blue Sky Press.

Henderson, Kathy. 2004. *And the good brown earth.* Cambridge, MA: Candlewick Press.

Hoberman, Mary Ann, and Jane Dyer. 2004. *Whose garden is it?* Orlando: Gulliver Books/ Harcourt.

Jordan, Helene J., and Loretta Krupinski. 1992. *How a seed grows.* New York: HarperCollins.

Medearis, Angela Shelf, and Jill Dubin. 1999. *Seeds grow!* New York: Scholastic.

Oram, Hiawyn, and Susan Varley. 2000. *Princess Chamomile's garden.* New York: Dutton Children's Books.

Rockwell, Anne F. 1999. *Bumblebee, bumblebee, do you know me? A garden guessing game.* New York: HarperCollins.

Pond, Creek, or Stream Walk

Before the Walk

Water is not only fascinating to children, but is a magnet for all forms of living things, which makes ponds, creeks, and streams wonderful places to observe nature and enhance children's learning about the world around them. Prior to visiting a pond, creek, or stream with the children, find out what they already know about these types of water environments or what they might be interested in learning about them. Research pond, creek, or stream ecosystems and share what you discover with the children, emphasizing their delicate balance—how all plants and creatures depend on one another for survival—and how easy it is to disrupt that balance.

For children who are unfamiliar with these types of water habitats, read a variety of picture books to give them a foundation for learning. Introduce a few new vocabulary words younger children might use during the walk. Words are much more meaningful to young children if they can connect the words with real-life objects, situations, or concepts. Throughout the year, the children can study these rich water environments to

- observe the comings and goings of living creatures that frequent these bodies of water
- feed the ducks and frogs
- look for and learn about the plants that grow nearby
- consider why so many things grow in ponds, creeks, and streams
- notice ripples (cause and effect) from tossing things in the pond
- collect water and small creatures from the pond to examine more closely

Words to Use and Learn

algae	duck	log	snail
cattail	fish	pond	stream
creek	frog	reed	water
dam	lake	ripple	weed
dragonfly	lily pad	river	wetland

Things to Bring on the Walk

✓ a spiral notebook that includes the children's questions and any notes about experiences that might interest them (provocations), and for noting your observations of the children during the walk

✓ a camera

✓ notebooks and paper for the children

✓ writing and drawing tools

✓ backpacks, containers, or plastic and paper bags for collecting things

✓ magnifying glasses

✓ dried bread crumbs or stale bread

✓ water-habitats reference guide

✓ a tape recorder or other recording device

✓ pool-cleaning net or similar type of net

✓ one or two gallon-size ice-cream tubs or other empty container(s)

During the Walk

Consider using some of the following suggestions during the walk to help children learn about ponds, creeks, or streams. Should children discover other aspects that interest them, be sure to help them pursue and later document those interests.

Observing Quietly

When you arrive at your destination, begin by telling the children about the importance of quiet observation. In natural habitats, you often see and hear much more if you remain quiet and limit your motions. Wild creatures are typically not used to people, and may hide or stop what they are doing if they sense others around. That is just their way of protecting themselves.

Stand and watch the pond, creek, or stream. Are there any ducks, birds, or turtles? Are there any bugs or other signs of animal life? Does the water move or is it still?

Notice plant life on or by the pond, such as cattails, lily pads, or weeds. Are there trees, roots, or fallen branches by the pond? Are things growing on them? Are there signs of animal life around the plants, such as frogs or tadpoles?

What colors do you see in the pond? Is the water all the same color or does it change? Wonder what causes any green color on the pond. Walk along and see what other things you notice about the pond.

Throw some bread crumbs on the water and along the shore and watch how the ducks go after them. Do some ducks get more than others?

  Using the Senses

Invite the children to take deep breaths. What do they smell? What might cause the smells? Are there many different smells, some good, others bad?

What words describe how it feels to be by the pond, creek, or stream? Write down the words the children use to express their feelings. Have older children write down their own words.

Listen to sounds around the pond. Find a spot to sit and have everyone close their eyes and listen. Do they hear sounds in the water or from small creatures near the water?

Identifying Plants

Use reference guides to help you name some of the things you see in the pond. Let the children name some of the plants they know and look up some of the others. Write the names down. Older children can keep their own lists and note their own observations. Also consider keeping a list of everything seen at the pond, creek, or stream, if possible.

Call attention to characteristics that can help you identify things later on after the walk (for example, flat round leaves in the water, feathery-type shoots from clumps of grass, droopy-type branches hanging over the pond, unknown birds).

Collecting Samples

Use the gallon ice-cream bucket or other container to collect some water from the pond. Use a magnifying glass to study the water for anything children can't see with their eyes alone. Are there things they can see, such as snails or water beetles?

Bring back the water samples if they look interesting, and observe them over the next few days for signs of life. If possible, bring back samples of different plants, tree bark, or small branches growing around the water environment. Let the children help carry the small, nonspillable samples.

Some Safety Notes

Be extremely cautious with children around water, and practice water safety at all times. Show the children exactly how far to stand from the water—use markers if necessary. Only adults should collect samples from the pond, creek, or stream; the children can inspect the collected samples away from the water's edge. Toss food into the water or leave it on the shore for ducks and birds. Walking around ponds, creeks, and streams can also provide opportunities for discussing ecology and the importance of sustaining all natural habitats.

 **After the Walk**

After returning from the walk, talk about all the things seen around the water environment. Examine anything collected such as water samples. Discuss pond, creek, or stream ecosystems again, emphasizing things seen or heard during the walk. Write down questions the children may have about the water environment they observed and work with them to discover the answers.

Older Children

The older children in your group may be inspired to create a large mural of the pond, creek, or stream they observed. Be sure to print any photos you may have taken for the children's reference in constructing the mural. Have books, such as reference books or books read prior to the walk, available for their reference as well. Some supplies to use include brown craft paper or white table-cover paper, and scrap materials, such as construction paper, tissue paper, plastic bubble wrap, and pieces of brown and green plastic (such as garbage bags). Add colored tape or yarn and small paste sticks to use for streams, fencing, or bridges. Provide magazine pictures, wallpaper samples, and glue, as well as tempera paints, brushes, markers, and crayons. Keep a collection of dried weeds, cattails, twigs, bark, and things brought back.

Wildlife journals and notebooks are a wonderful way to record one's thoughts and observations about the natural world. They often include sketches as well as text. Show the children some examples of wildlife journals and encourage them to begin keeping their own journals starting with their walk to the pond, creek, or stream.

Invite the children to select one or two animals, birds, insects, or plants they saw during the walk to research. The children can use their findings to create short nonfiction or fiction pieces about their chosen topics.

Have the children write letters to local or national conservation organizations. In their letters, have them describe what they saw and learned during their walk and why it is important to protect these kinds of environments for future generations.

Consider returning every month or so to the water environment you visited and have the children note how the pond, creek, or stream has changed over the weeks. Children can note the changes in their wildlife journals.

Younger Children

What types of things did the children collect from the walk, and how might they use them to demonstrate their learning? Remember that tactile experiences are how young children learn best, so consider inviting children to spread out their collections on a table or two for the group to examine together or to look at water samples brought back from the walk. While the children explore the items, ask open-ended questions that encourage them to think about the items and their observations of the pond, creek, or stream. Then guide them to consider how they might use materials in the room or outside to demonstrate for others some aspect of their learning about water environments.

Create a class story on chart paper about "A Day in the Life of a Pond (or Creek or Stream)." Invite each child to share something she remembers from the walk. Each thing a child mentions will become a page in the class book. For children who are writing, encourage them to write their words on a blank page and then draw pictures to accompany them. Work with other children to write exactly what they say on their own page and encourage them to draw pictures too.

Add new words related to the walk to an existing word wall.

Find items in the room that are the same as things seen during the walk, such as a toy fish, a toy duck, a plant, and water (either in a fishbowl or from the faucet). Create labels for the items and display them near where the items are in the room or on the items themselves, if possible. Be sure to call children's attention to the items you have labeled and how they are spelled.

Create a list of at least five things seen during the walk. Then visit your local library or bookseller to locate books related to those things, such as books about ponds, ducks, and water habitats. Read each book you found to the children.

 **Revisiting the Walk**

Return to the pond, creek, or stream you visited during each season of the year. Before returning, however, discuss with the children some of the things they observed last time. Encourage them to look for the same things during the new walk.

Or consider inviting a wildlife expert to accompany you during the next walk. Before the walk, help children compile a list of questions they may want to ask the visitor.

Books

Arnosky, Jin. 2002. *All about frogs.* New York: Scholastic.

———. 2008. *The brook book: Exploring the smallest streams.* New York: Dutton Children's Books.

Baker, Nick. 2007. *Rivers, ponds, and lakes.* New York: HarperCollins.

Beatty, Richard. 2003. *Rivers, lakes, streams, and ponds.* Austin, TX: Raintree Steck-Vaughn.

Donovan, Sandra. 2002. *Animals of rivers, lakes, and ponds.* Austin: Raintree Steck-Vaughn.

Fleming, Denise. 1993. *In the small, small pond.* New York: H. Holt.

Hunter, Anne. 1999. *What's in the pond?* Boston: Houghton Mifflin.

Lindeen, Carol. 2003. *Life in a stream.* Mankato, MN: Capstone Press.

Morrison, Gordon. 2006. *A drop of water.* Boston: Houghton Mifflin.

Parker, Steve, and Philip Dowell. 2005. *Eyewitness pond & river.* New York: Dorling Kindersley.

Pascoe, Elaine, and Dwight Kuhn. 2003. *The ecosystem of a stream.* New York: PowerKids Press.

Rockwell, Anne F., and Lizzy Rockwell. 1994. *Ducklings and pollywogs.* New York: Macmillan.

Royston, Angela. 2005. *Rivers.* Chicago: Heinemann Library.

Taylor, Barbara. 2000. *Pond and river life.* Hauppauge, NY: Barron's Educational Series.

Wechsler, Doug. 2006. *Frog heaven: Ecology of a vernal pool.* Honesdale, PA: Boyds Mills Press.

Community Walks

"We go to the playground and Vivian went down the slide"
Ian, age 4

Hotel/Motel Walk

Before the Walk

In our mobile society, many people consider staying in a hotel or motel a routine activity. Young children, however, may have no idea what kind of place a parent is referring to as either a potential vacation stop or a stopover on a business trip. A visit to a hotel or motel expands children's firsthand knowledge of a place they may have only heard about. Even older children with experience staying in hotels or motels may discover a lot they didn't know about these "homes away from home."

It is best to visit a hotel or motel site prior to walking with the children to get an idea of the special features to look for and point out to them. Look for hotels with suites and special attractions, such as a glass elevator over an atrium garden. Also, you may need to obtain permission to tour certain parts of a hotel or motel, so be sure to inquire about that during your previsit as well. Since this type of facility may not be accustomed to hosting field trips for young children, the staff may not realize they have anything of interest to offer. Explain to the manager why you want to visit and what you would like to show the children.

Ask the children in advance how many of them have stayed in a hotel or motel or have visited someone they knew who was staying in a hotel. What do they remember about it? What kinds of things do you need to take with you when you stay in a hotel? Do you need to take blankets, pillows, sleeping bags, towels, or just things you want to have? Can you bring pets? How will you get everything into your room? Write down the children's questions and try to answer them during the walk.

Note

The primary distinction between a hotel and a motel is that hotel rooms open to an inside hallway, and motel rooms open to the outside. Adjust the suggestions of activities based on whether your walk involves a hotel or motel.

A visit to a nearby hotel or motel can offer children opportunities to

- learn about the different jobs people do in hotels
- notice where people eat and sleep in hotels
- observe how the building and the rooms look and how they are maintained
- consider what other services or facilities are available in hotels
- study how various things work, such as room keys, elevators, and luggage carts
- wonder how hotels may be similar to homes and how they are different

Words to Use and Learn

check-in	hallway	key/key card	reservation
check-out	hotel	lobby	room number
elevator	housekeeping	motel	swimming pool
escalator	ice machine	parking lot	vacancy
exit	inn	registration desk	vending machine

Things to Bring on the Walk

✓ a spiral notebook that includes the children's questions and notes about experiences that might interest them (provocations), and for noting your observations of the children during the walk

✓ a camera

✓ notebooks for the children

✓ writing and drawing tools

✓ backpacks or paper bags for collecting things

✓ a tape recorder or other recording device

During the Walk

Refresh your memory about the types of questions children asked about hotels and remember to try to answer their questions during the walk at the hotel. Use the following ideas to engage the children while at the hotel or motel.

Identifying First Impressions
What is the hotel's name? Sometimes hotels are named for important citizens from the past. As you arrive, notice parking areas and how they function. Is there a loading and unloading area in front of the hotel? Point out the lines that tell people where to park. Is there a doorman? What is the doorman wearing? What do doormen do?

Notice the size and shape of the building. Can you tell from the outside how many floors it has?

How can people tell whether there is room to stay at the hotel? Is there a sign outside or do they have to go in and ask? Notice any plantings, decorations around the building, flags, or banners. Is there a theme to the decoration? Are there play areas, a pool, or other special attractions outdoors? Who uses them? Discuss why some hotels or motels offer these things.

Do you see people arriving at or leaving the hotel? Does anyone help them with their luggage? How do travelers transport their luggage? Point out the special luggage carts (if not in use) and how they are suited for carrying different types of baggage from hanging garment bags to bulky duffel bags.

What's Inside the Front Door?
Notice the lobby and reception area, including the decorations and furniture. Are there any large plants or chandeliers? Is the style of decoration related to the hotel's name? Invite children to locate posted schedules, directories, or maps in the lobby.

Watch people check in and out at the reception desk. How can you tell if they're checking in or checking out? Are room keys or key cards visible, perhaps in numbered boxes behind the desk? Ask at the desk to visit a room and demonstrate the use of keys or key cards.

Are there machines in the desk area? How many people are behind the desk and what are they doing? Do the phones ring a lot?

Is there a concierge desk in the lobby? What does a concierge do?

Notice other hotel employees in the lobby and what they are doing to serve guests and keep the hotel clean and efficient. Are there bellboys? What do bellboys do?

What Else Happens in Hotels?
Walk around other public and private areas of the hotel. Are there meeting rooms or places to sit, eat, shop, play, or exercise? Are there decorations or artwork in these areas?

Find a hallway that contains rooms. Notice how long the hallway is, its exit signs, stairways, elevators, room numbers (and room numbers in Braille), as well as anything else of interest.

Do the children see housekeepers or housekeeping carts? Investigate the housekeeping carts. What do housekeeping carts contain? Invite older children to make a list of the things on housekeeping carts. Talk about what a big job it would be to clean all these rooms every day. Consider asking a housekeeper what she does when she cleans a room and how many rooms she cleans each day. If you did not get a key or key card from the front desk, ask a housekeeping person if she can show you how the keys or key cards work in the doors. Ask if you can look inside a room. Invite children to notice the furniture, lamps, artwork, closets, TVs, telephones, and special items, such as coffee makers and ice buckets. Look in several rooms if possible. Is each room the same or different?

Look for an ice machine and show children how it works. Are there other vending machines in the area? What do they contain?

Using the Senses

Revisit the lobby and have the children use other senses to experience it. What aromas do the children smell in the hotel lobby? Is the restaurant nearby and do they smell food? Has the floor been recently cleaned and do the children smell items used for cleaning?

Invite children to close their eyes and listen to the sounds around them. What do they hear? Other people moving around? Fountains? People talking? Elevator bells? Phones ringing?

Exploring Elevators

If there is a glass elevator, watch the elevator go up and down. Take a few rides on elevators. How does it feel to go up and down?

What Would You Do If . . . ?

- you forgot the number of your room?
- you lost your room key?
- your luggage went to the wrong room?
- you forgot your toothbrush or hairbrush?
- the TV wasn't working?
- your room was too hot or cold or noisy?

Taking Photographs

Take photographs throughout the walk—from approaching the front door to leaving the hotel. Ask hotel staff if you can take their photographs too.

Asking Questions

Have the children's questions about hotels been answered? What new questions do they have? Consider asking the following questions:

? Where does all the laundry get washed? Where are linens and supplies kept? Are there extra beds or cribs for baby guests? (Perhaps a housekeeper can show you where these things are kept.)

? Why might there be trays outside some of the rooms? Do the children know what *room service* means? How do kitchen staff know what kinds of food to prepare? Where is the hotel kitchen? (Perhaps the catering office or someone in the restaurant can tell you.)

? What is different about staying in a hotel versus staying at your home or someone else's home?

After the Walk

Did the children collect anything from the hotel walk? Invite them to share and discuss what they collected. Listen to what they say about the walk. Use their thoughts and ideas as starting points for things they may choose to document about their walk through the hotel.

Share the digital photos with the children or make copies of the photographs as soon as possible.

Older Children

Encourage children to use their imaginations in thinking about how to document what they learned from the walk. For example, if your program had a concierge, what would her responsibilities be? Children who can read and write might consider writing a classified ad for a "Program Concierge" that lists all job requirements and responsibilities. Children may even try out being the program's concierge for a day.

For children interested in interior design, provide materials such as fabric swatches, paint color samples, and interior design magazines. Encourage them to design a hotel lobby that incorporates examples of furniture style and fabric and any special features, such as a pond, glass elevators, and skylights.

Have children write stories about one of the people they saw at the hotel or motel. Children can title their books "A Day in the Life of a Bellboy" or "A Day in the Life of a Cashier."

Give children blank index cards to make postcards. On one side of the postcard, children can draw a picture of a hotel or motel. On the other side, they can write a message to a family member or friend telling the person about the wonderful time they are having at the hotel. (Wish you were here!)

Have children write a play about an event that happens at a hotel or motel, such as a comedy involving mixed-up luggage or a mystery involving a missing room key. Children can even collect costumes and other props and perform the play for others.

On chart paper, work with the children to create a list of all the words they can think of related to hotels or motels. Then challenge the children to create a short story or poem using all of the words on the list.

Younger Children

Children who may never have visited a hotel before may be very excited about the many things they observed about hotels. Try to determine what about hotels fascinated them most. Some children may have been very interested in a glass elevator or large fountain in the lobby. What was it about those things they enjoyed most? Going up and down in the elevator? The shimmering colors and splashing water of the fountain? Perhaps they were intrigued by the housekeeping cart. What would a housekeeping cart for cleaning their rooms at home contain? Consider having children use small boxes such as shoe boxes or tissue boxes to create and fill their own housekeeping carts.

Set up the dramatic play area to look like a hotel or motel. Use items such as a desk and chair, a toy telephone and cash register, a box with keys, other chairs and small tables (to create a lobby), suitcases, and dress-up clothes. Children can then role-play different scenarios using the props.

Add new words related to hotels or motels to an existing word wall.

With the children, write a group story about the walk to a hotel or motel on chart paper. To encourage children to contribute to the story, ask them open-ended questions to help them recall the walk, for example, "What did the person at the desk tell us?" or "Where did the man take the cart full of luggage?"

Give children white paper plates and ask them to draw pictures of the food they would order from room service if they stayed in a hotel. Then invite children to tell others what they ordered from room service.

 ## Revisiting the Walk

Do the children have any remaining questions about hotels or the people who work there? If you revisit the hotel, try setting up in advance a time when children can ask questions of various hotel employees, such as the concierge, the host in the restaurant, or a bellboy. Work with the children in advance to create a list of questions for the people they interview.

Books

Brewster, Patience. 1991. *Rabbit Inn*. Boston: Little, Brown.

Cheshire, Marc, Carolyn Bracken, and Hilary Knight. 2005. *Here comes Eloise!* A lift-the-flap book. Kay Thompson's Eloise. New York: Little Simon.

Cushman, Doug. 1992. *Aunt Eater's mystery vacation*. New York: HarperCollins.

Diviny, Sean, and Joe Rocco. 2000. *Halloween Motel*. New York: HarperCollins.

Florian, Douglas. 1993. *Monster Motel: Poems and paintings*. San Diego: Harcourt Brace Jovanovich.

Labatt, Mary. 2001. *A weekend at the Grand Hotel*. Toronto, ON: Kids Can Press.

McClatchy, Lisa, Tammie Lyon, and Kay Thompson. 2007. *Eloise's new bonnet*. Kay Thompson's Eloise. New York: Aladdin.

Napoli, Donna Jo, Shelagh Johnston, and Kenneth J. Spengler. 2004. *Hotel Jungle*. New York: Mondo.

Okimoto, Jean Davies, and Howie Schneider. 1990. *Blumpoe the Grumpoe meets Arnold the Cat*. Boston: Joy Street Books.

Pinkwater, Daniel Manus, and Jill Pinkwater. 1997. *At the Hotel Larry*. New York: Marshall Cavendish.

Schwarz, Laurence, and Kelly Denato. 2006. *Ellen's 11-star spectacular super deluxe hotel*. New York: Little, Brown.

Thompson, Kay, Mart Crowley, and Hilary Knight. 2002. *Kay Thompson's Eloise takes a bawth*. New York: Simon & Schuster Books for Young Readers.

Thompson, Kay, and Hilary Knight. 2001. *Eloise in Paris*. London: Simon & Schuster.

Vaughan, Marcia K., and Patricia Mullins. 1995. *The Sea-Breeze Hotel*. Sydney: Margaret Hamilton Books.

Waber, Bernard. 1995. *Do you see a mouse?* Boston: Houghton Mifflin.

Library Walk

Before the Walk

Public libraries are valuable community resources and are great walking destinations for children. Libraries are child-friendly places with many interesting items to observe and explore. Before your trip to the library, find out whether any children have been to libraries before. Show them your library card and ask if any of them have library cards. Explain to the children that a library card allows you to check out books and other materials from the library to take home or to your center or school.

A visit to the library offers children opportunities to

- attend story hour, a puppet show, or a special program
- get a library card and check out books and other items

- look up specific information they may want to know
- look for something in magazines or newspapers from other places
- learn about how the library works and what the people who work there do

A library is a perfect site for an initial walking trip. It is appropriate for most age groups and for mixed age groups. Small groups can visit a library informally using many of the ideas suggested in this section (there are enough suggestions here for several trips). If you bring a large group or want to visit special parts of the library, schedule a more formal tour. Many libraries have community rooms that you can reserve in advance for your group's use. Libraries can and should be visited many different times to fully explore the rich resources they offer.

Words to Use and Learn

author	cassette tapes	fiction	reference
bar code	CDs	librarian	return
book	check-out	magazines	scanner
book drop	computer catalog	newspapers	shelves
call and catalog numbers	dictionary	nonfiction	stacks

Things to Bring on the Walk

✓ a spiral notebook that includes the children's questions and notes about experiences that might interest them (provocations), and for noting your observations of the children during the walk

✓ a camera

✓ backpacks or paper bags for collecting things

✓ paper

✓ writing and drawing tools

✓ your library card, or information needed to apply for one

✓ a tape recorder or other recording device

During the Walk

The following activity suggestions are some of the learning opportunities available to children at the library. It is likely the children will also come up with their own questions or ideas of things to do while they are in the library.

Outside the Library

Notice the setting of the library and its building. Is it a big, imposing building with many steps and statues around it, a more modern structure with large glass windows, or a small neighborhood library? Talk about any artwork you see around the outside of the building. Are there inviting places to read outside by the building? If so, think about bringing a blanket on your next visit to have an outdoor story time.

Notice the name of the library and explain any significance it might have. Is this the main library or a branch? Explain that libraries are so important and helpful that there are many of them in communities to make them easy for people to get to and use.

Look for a cornerstone on the building to see the date when the library was built. Why is there a flag in front of the library?

Look at the hours printed on the door. When does the library open? Can people bring things back to the library when it is closed? Notice drop boxes people can use when the library is closed.

Wonder how people get to this library. How can you tell? Is there a parking lot for cars and bike racks for bikes, or is this library in a big city with bus or transit stops nearby?

Take photographs of the library both on the outside and inside.

Inside the Library (General Areas)

Once inside notice special displays, exhibits, artwork, or decorations. Are there themes to the displays you can help the children understand? What kinds of things are on the walls? Are there special books on display? Is there information about the library and a library map or guide to show the children? What other information is available for people to take with them?

Notice how the library is organized. Look at the central checkout and return area, and the computers and information desks where you can get help. Point out the equipment on the checkout counter and how the people behind the counter handle each book. Many libraries have an automated circulation system that uses a laser beam. Explain that the laser beam records the number of the book and the number on the library card and tells the computer system that someone is checking out the book. Some libraries still use photocopying equipment to keep track of who has checked out each book. Show the children where to put books that are being returned and explain that the librarians will copy the number again to show that the book has been returned.

Visit the reference area of the library and show the children all the encyclopedias, dictionaries, almanacs, and other reference books. Look up the topic of your questions in an encyclopedia, or ask the reference librarian for help. Show the children the many volumes of the *Readers' Guide to Periodical Literature*, which lists all the articles in magazines by topics. Explain that reference materials stay in the library so anyone can come to look for answers to their questions. Notice that there are many places to sit and work in the reference area.

Visit the newspaper and magazine area (called *periodicals*) and notice how everything is displayed. Are there comfortable chairs for people to sit and read? Look at the newspapers hanging on their special racks and notice the name of the city in the newspaper headings. If there are maps or globes in this area, point out some locations. Show the children the special machines that people can use to read newspaper and magazine articles stored on microfilm or microfiche. Copying information on microfiche helps the library save old newspapers and other periodicals using very little space.

Compare all the different types of library shelves, racks, and containers, and think about how they are suited to the items they hold. Some examples of shelves include the newspaper and magazine racks; small paperback book racks; big, solid shelves for heavy reference materials; smaller shelves for videos, DVDs, and CDs; tall shelves in the adult area; and lower shelves in the children's area.

Notice the signs around the library that tell what is in each section. Read them to the children and discuss what they mean. Particularly notice the signs on shelves that say *fiction* and *nonfiction*, since those are the categories that are crucial to how libraries are organized.

Explain that *fiction* means stories that are made up, such as the *Curious George* books. *Nonfiction* means books about real things in the world, such as the First Discovery Series of books. Storybooks (fiction) are organized by the author's last name. They are in alphabetical order on the shelves. All other books are organized by number and kind of book. The librarian can explain how your library is organized.

Visiting the Children's Area

Wonder how people find the books they want when they go to the library. Do they browse around until they find something they like, or look up a book in the catalog and go find it?

Let the children browse in the children's area and choose books to look at. Show the children the letters on the shelves and see whether they match the first letters of the author's last name. Those must be fiction books.

Point out the numbers on the books. Both numbers and letters may be printed on the edge of the book. This is the book's call number and is something like a person's address. It is how libraries keep track of their books. Look inside the back cover of the book. Is there a pocket with a card in it with numbers printed on it, or is there a label with a bunch of black stripes and numbers on it? If the book has the stripes, your library is computerized and uses a bar code system. Many books will have both; pockets left from their older system and the bar code labels of their new system.

Notice whether the children's area has special sections for very large books, regular books, and cassette tapes or CDs. Are there toys, stuffed animals, or puppets to play with? Is there a place for storytelling or puppet shows? Are there computers, CD players, or DVD players?

Notice how the area is decorated and whether there are special displays. Does the library have programs for children?

Explain to the children that in the library they may leave books on the table or put them in a special bin. They should not try to put them back on the shelf because each book has its own place on the shelf. Librarians can put the books back for them.

Wondering about Libraries
How do people reach things that are high up? Are there step stools, ladders, or special tools to reach things?

How does the library take care of its books to help them last? Notice the paper or plastic jackets that cover many books. Can a library employee show you how they make the book jackets and put them on books, or do the books come already covered?

How do people repair books that get torn? Is there a special work area for fixing books? What do the employees use? What does the library do with the books that are worn out or out of date? Do you see any books for sale?

What happens when people don't return their books on time? Are there fines for overdue or damaged books? How do the librarians decide what books to order for the library? Where do the books arrive and how do librarians get them ready to put on the shelves?

After the Walk

When you are back from the walk, talk about the walk to the library and ask the children to tell you all the things they noticed and remembered. Write down their comments on a large sheet of paper. Refer to the list later if children need more ideas about how to demonstrate their learning about libraries.

Older Children
Did you notice what was most interesting to the older children about the visit to the library? Do they think they could make a replica of the library and its general areas using a shoe box or in a

drawing? If that seems interesting to them, gather materials for them to use.

Ask the children to think about what would happen if suddenly there weren't any libraries. Could they write a story or a play about a world without libraries? What would that world look like? What would people do without books or things to read?

Ask the children if the library in the program's room looks like a library. Why or why not? What could they do to the group's library to make it more like the library you visited? Could they have storytelling events for the younger children, just like at real libraries?

Invite the children to explore book making. If they could make books, what kinds of books would they make? Gather materials and have the children make their own special types of books.

Have the children think about all of the things that happen in libraries each day.

Do any children have a favorite author? If the author(s) is still alive, encourage the children to write letters to him or her, explaining what they like best about the books. If an author is deceased, it is still sometimes possible to write to the publisher; a representative may write back on behalf of the author.

Younger Children

Younger children enjoy simply holding books. Consider helping children create their own board books from tagboard or cardboard. Children can scribble in their books or glue things inside them. This would also be an opportunity to discuss how to treat books so pages aren't torn and the books aren't ruined. You could use their board books to demonstrate how to hold books when reading, for example, pages are turned from right to left, and we read from left to right.

Younger children can also be involved in helping the older children transform the group's library to look more like a real library. Be sure to involve them in the activity if implemented. .

Bring in interesting magazine pictures and show them to the children. Decide what topic each picture is about and put them in file folders with the name of the topic on it. Use letters or a picture- or number-code system to organize the picture file so the children can learn to find the pictures they are looking for.

Give children materials for making their own library cards to use in the group's library. Some children may even enjoy role-playing a librarian and helping other children check out books.

Create a letter-display table using small objects that begin with a particular letter. For example, for C, display a toy car, a plastic toy cookie, a toy crab, and a comb. Store the objects in small boxes. When you have collections for several letters, set up a letter file system in a hardware organizer case (a thirty-drawer case works well). Put a letter sticker on each drawer and keep it on the letter-display table. Have children put the objects in the appropriate letter drawer after they have used them.

Revisiting the Walk

Before you visit the library again, work with the children to make a big book about your visits. Include in the book what you saw on display, what you did there, and some new thing you learned about the library. Add to your book each time you go to the library and date each entry. Include pictures you took and add the children's writing and drawings.

Books

Caseley, Judith. 1993. *Sophie and Sammy's library sleepover.* New York: Greenwillow Books.

Flanagan, Alice K., and Christine Osinski. 1996. *Ms. Davison, our librarian.* New York: Children's Press.

Gibbons, Gail. 1988. *Check it out! The book about libraries.* Orlando: Harcourt.

Hill, Lee Sullivan. 1997. *Libraries take us far.* Minneapolis: Carolrhoda Books.

Huff, Barbara A., and Iris Van Rynbach. 1990. *Once inside the library.* Boston: Little, Brown.

Johnston, Marianne. 2000. *Let's visit the library.* New York: Power Kids Press.

Knudsen, Michelle, and Kevin Hawkes. 2006. *Library lion.* Cambridge, MA: Candlewick Press.

Liebman, Daniel. 2003. *I want to be a librarian.* Toronto, ON: Firefly Books.

Miller, Heather. 2003. *Librarian.* Chicago: Heinemann Library.

Morris, Ann, and Peter Linenthal. 2003. *That's our librarian!* Brookfield, CT: Millbrook Press.

Ready, Dee. 1998. *Librarians.* Mankato, MN: Bridgestone Books.

Ruurs, Margriet. 2005. *My librarian is a camel: How books are brought to children around the world.* Honesdale, PA: Boyds Mills Press.

Shea, Kitty, and Zachary Trover. 2006. *Out and about at the public library.* Minneapolis: Picture Window Books.

Simon, Charnan, and Rebecca McKillip Thornburgh. 2007. *Lewis the librarian. Magic door to learning.* Chanhassen, MN: The Child's World.

Sweeney, Alyce. 2007. *Welcome to the library.* New York: Children's Press/Scholastic.

Bakery Walk

Before the Walk

Bakeries tend to be places of interest to children and most children have either been to a bakery or to the bakery section in a grocery store. Additionally, many children are likely to have had experiences baking or eating baked goods in their own homes. Prior to a walk to a bakery, consider the ages and interests of the children in your group. Local neighborhood bakeries tend to be small gathering places, so it may be best to discuss your trip beforehand with the bakery owners. If there is a commercial bakery within walking distance of your center, set up a tour beforehand, making sure the tour leader is aware of the ages of the children in your group so he or she can tailor the tour accordingly. Keep in mind that commercial bakeries contain heavy machinery and can be noisy, and that bakery ovens are potentially dangerous for active children. That said, bakeries offer many rich learning opportunities for children of all ages.

A visit to a nearby bakery can provide children opportunities to

- observe and consider the physical changes in materials, such as smooth dough becoming warm, crusty loaves of bread

- learn the names of various machinery and equipment used in bakeries and what they do

- talk about measurement concepts

- discover where different baking ingredients come from

- notice that people in bakeries have specific jobs and that it takes many people doing their part to produce large quantities of baked goods

Prior to the walk, find out what children know about baked goods and how they are produced. For example, ask younger children where the bread they eat for lunch comes from or who makes the cupcakes they see in stores. Ask older children what they know about bakery jobs and the equipment used in larger bakeries. Make a list of questions the children have about bakeries and be sure to bring your list with you during the walk.

Words to Use and Learn

bake	dough	mix	scale
baked goods	dry ingredients	oven	sifter
baker	flour*	pastry/pastry chef	spatula
batter	ingredients		stale
cool	measuring cups and spoons	pie/pie pan	wet ingredients
		rolling pin	

*Make sure children understand the difference between "flour" used for baking and the "flowers" they see growing outdoors.

Things to Bring on the Walk

✓ a spiral notebook that includes the children's questions and notes about experiences that might interest them (provocations), and for noting your observations of the children during the walk

✓ writing and drawing tools

✓ clipboards and paper for the children

✓ backpacks or paper bags for collecting things

✓ a camera

✓ a tape recorder or other recording device

During the Walk

Consider using some of the following suggestions during the walk to help the children learn about bakeries. Should children discover other aspects of the bakery that interest them, be sure to help them pursue and later document those interests.

Observing at Bakeries

Notice the appearance of the bakery and the area around it. If it is a large commercial bakery, is there a parking lot in front? Where is the name of the bakery? What is the entry into the bakery like? Is there a waiting area? Do you have to sign in for a tour? Are there display cases in the entry area? Are there photographs of the facility? Do they show what the original bakery looked like? Who first started the bakery? Is the bakery named for anyone in particular? What are the hours of the bakery? What are the hours of the employees? Children may be surprised to learn how early most bakery employees arrive at work each morning. Ask them why people who work in bakeries have to arrive so early for work. How many employees can you see in the entry area?

If it is a small bakery, do most people walk to the bakery or is there a parking area nearby? What is the name of the bakery? Is the bakery named for anyone in particular or does the name reflect baking or baked goods? What is the entry into the bakery like? Are there tables for sitting? How many? Can you see the kitchen from the entry or the sitting area? Where are the display cases? Where is the cashier and cash register? Do you have to take a number to be waited on? Is there a board with daily specials? What are the hours of the bakery? Where are they posted? When do the

employees have to arrive at the bakery each day? What other items does the bakery sell besides baked goods?

What do the display cases contain? Are the prices near each item? Are some items priced individually and by the dozen? Is there an area for discounted items, such as items that were baked the day before? How much cheaper are they than the freshly baked items?

How big is the kitchen? What kinds of equipment does the kitchen contain? How many ovens are in the kitchen? How many racks are in the kitchen? Is there proofing and fermentation equipment? (In bakery terminology, "proofing" refers to activating yeast by mixing it with water and sugar or milk.) Are there cookie machines? Are there mixers, bowls, and measuring tools? Where are they kept? What do the bakers use to remove hot items from the ovens? What do they wear on their hands? Is some of the equipment heavy? What other kinds of machinery and equipment are in the kitchen? Are there any machines or baking utensils children do not know the names of? Is there a sink and a refrigerator in the kitchen? What might be kept in the refrigerator? Where are the dry ingredients kept? How big are the bags of flour, sugar, and other dry ingredients? Where are the bakery boxes kept? Are there certificates or legal documents on the walls? Are there recipes on the walls? Is it bright in the kitchen? Is it warm in the kitchen?

What are the different jobs people have in bakeries? What types of clothing do they wear?

Do they wear special hats? Are there items of clothing they must wear by law? What are they? Do some people specialize in certain jobs, such as pastry chef or cake decorator? How do people learn these jobs?

How many different kinds of the same items does the bakery produce, such as cookies, cakes, and pies? Which items do they sell the most of?

  ## Using the Senses

What does a bakery smell like? Do you smell bread, cookies, or cake? Close your eyes and see if you can tell what you smell. Are there other smells besides baked goods, such as coffee? Ask the children what words they would use to describe the smell of a bakery.

What sounds do you hear in the bakery? Do you hear timers going off? Do you hear bakers calling things out to one another? Does the cashier call out people's numbers in line? Is the phone ringing?

Are there free samples for you to taste?

Categorizing and Counting
Depending on the ages of the children in your group, they may enjoy counting the number of

- total items in the display cases
- different items in the cases, such as cakes, cookies, and donuts, and how many there are of each item
- different types of the same thing in the display cases, such as different kinds of donuts, cookies, and bagels
- items in the kitchen, such as ovens and racks

Collecting Items
Ask if there are any old displays, pictures of baked goods, or other throwaways that might be useful to the children, such as in the dramatic play area or in the block area.

Asking Questions

If you are on a special tour of a commercial bakery, ask

? How many employees work at the bakery?

? What clothing items are employees required to wear?

? When do most employees come to work and when do they leave for the day?

? How many of the different items does the bakery produce in a day and in a week?

? Where does the bakery sells its baked goods?

? Where does the bakery gets its baking supplies such as flour, sugar, and butter? How much of those types of items does the bakery use in a week?

? Which baked goods are the most difficult to produce and why?

? May we take photographs of the kitchen or of employees baking?

 **After the Walk**

Discuss the trip to the bakery with the children and what they remember about the visit. Did they learn anything about bakeries that they didn't know before? What would it be like to work in a bakery? Show the children photographs taken during the walk and ask them what was happening in the various photos. Did the children bring back items that could be added to the dramatic play area or displayed in other areas of the room?

Older Children
Ask older children what interested them most about the bakery. Does working in a bakery seem like it would be a difficult job to perform? Why or why not? What would be some of the best things about working in a bakery? Where else might bakers work other than in bakeries? Do restaurants have bakers? Do hotels have bakers? Do some people operate their own bakery businesses from their homes?

People all over the world eat bread. Challenge the children to research different types of bread made worldwide. How many different types did they discover? Are some breads only baked for certain festivals or holidays? Why do they think bread is so popular worldwide?

Invite children to research baking techniques used now and long ago. What is the history of the oven? What were the very first ovens like? Are solar-powered ovens used anywhere in the world today? What are the latest features in oven design?

How many different baking terms are there? Create a list on chart paper of different baking terms including baking equipment and techniques. Invite children to create a dictionary of baking terminology.

There are literally thousands of recipes for baked goods, but how would children write recipes for concepts such as "love," "family," "home," or "friendship"? Invite children to create recipes for some of these concepts. For example, a recipe for friendship might include 4 cups of patience, 2 cups of understanding, and 4 cups of forgiveness. After they have written their recipes, ask children to share and discuss them with others.

Younger Children

Involve younger children in tactile experiences related to bakeries, such as creating baked goods from playdough they could sell in the group's "bakery," complete with prices.

Invite children to help paint a mural of a bakery that includes display cases, a customer-number dispenser, cash register, kitchen, and seating area. Hands-on experiences such as grinding wheat or actually making baked goods are excellent ways to reinforce young children's learning.

Add bakery-related words to an existing word wall.

Gather a variety of books from your local library or bookseller about breads from around the world. As you read the books to the children, keep a list of the different kinds of bread mentioned. If possible, purchase some of the breads for the children to taste. Invite the children to create drawings of the different breads and help them label the breads.

Ask the children and their families to share favorite cookie recipes. Collect the recipes and create a class cookbook of cookie recipes. As the children share their recipes, invite them to tell the group why the recipes are their favorites and how often they have the cookies at home. Have they ever helped make the cookies? Make copies of the cookbook for the children to illustrate and give to their families.

Have the children make baked-goods puppets from paper lunch bags, such as a pie puppet, cake puppet, or cinnamon-roll puppet. Then invite the children to put on puppet shows using their puppets. Encourage the children to consider what a cookie puppet might have to say to an apple-pie puppet. Where do the puppets live? Do the puppets like each other? Why or why not?

Revisiting the Walk

Next time you visit a bakery, try going at a different time of the day, such as an hour or so before the bakery closes. What is different about the bakery at that time of the day? Are there fewer items in the display cases? Have most of the employees gone home? Or focus on a different topic during the walk such as measurement concepts and measuring tools used for baking.

Books

Anderson, Catherine. 2005. *Bread bakery.* Chicago: Heineman Library.

Beck, Andrea. 1999. *Elliot bakes a cake.* Buffalo, NY: Kids Can Press.

Carle, Eric. 1995. *Walter the baker.* New York: Simon & Schuster.

Deedrick, Tami. 1998. *Bakers.* Mankato, MN: Bridgestone Books.

Dooley, Norah, and Peter J. Thornton. 1996. *Everybody bakes bread.* Minneapolis: Carolrhoda Books.

Ericsson, Jennifer A., and Anne McMullen. 2003. *Out and about at the bakery.* Minneapolis: Picture Window Books.

Flanagan, Alice K., and Romie Flanagan. 1998. *Mr. Santizo's tasty treats!* New York: Children's Press.

Greene, Carol, and Dann Penny. 1999. *At the bakery.* Chanhassen, MN: Child's World.

Harbison, Elizabeth M., and John Harbison. 1997. *Loaves of fun: A history of bread with activities and recipes from around the world.* Chicago: Chicago Review Press.

Hughes, Sarah. 2001. *My grandfather works in a bakery.* New York: Children's Press.

Morris, Ann, and Ken Heyman. 1993. *Bread, bread, bread.* New York: Scholastic.

Pickering, Robin. 2000. *I like bagels.* New York: Children's Press.

Rau, Dana Meachen. 2008. *Un panadero.* New York: Marshall Cavendish Benchmark.

Snyder, Inez. 2005. *Grains to bread.* New York: Children's Press.

Taus-Bolstad, Stacy. 2003. *From wheat to bread.* Minneapolis: Lerner Publications.

City Plaza Walk

Before the Walk

City plazas are fascinating places, and no two plazas are exactly alike. Some are enclosed and some are open air. Some include several decorative items, such as fountains. Since there is so much to see and do in plazas, the educational opportunities for children are practically endless. Be sure to preview the plaza to get an idea of possible focus areas for the walk before taking the children. However, be prepared to abandon your plans if something else is happening in the plaza that interests the children more.

Note
This walk could be adapted for a shopping mall if your program is not located in a city.

A walk through a city plaza offers children opportunities to

- observe different businesses and jobs
- notice the architecture and use of space in public venues
- discuss advertising techniques
- look for decorative features, such as fountains and plants, and wonder why they were included in the plaza decor
- consider the need for certain businesses in certain locations
- note what kinds of things are basic to most plazas, such as escalators and elevators and multiple sitting areas

Find out what the children already know about city plazas. What kinds of things might the children see in a city plaza? Make a list of the children's suggestions and bring it with you during the walk. Invite children to look for those things, and put a check mark next to the things you see on the list. Or make a list of pretend items to purchase at the plaza, such as shoes or CDs, and see whether there are stores that sell those things.

Words to Use and Learn

bench	escalator	lighting	sale
directory	exit sign	map	sculpture
displays	food court	restaurant	shops/shopper
drinking fountain	fountain	restroom	skylight
entrance sign	kiosk	retail store	statue

Things to Bring on the Walk

✓ a spiral notebook that includes the children's questions and notes about experiences that might interest them (provocations), and for noting your observations of the children during the walk

✓ writing and drawing tools

✓ clipboards and paper for the children

✓ a camera

✓ a tape recorder or other recording device

✓ backpacks or paper bags for collecting things

During the Walk

Consider using some of the following suggestions during the walk to help children learn about city plazas. Should children discover other aspects of the plaza that interest them, be sure to help them pursue and later document those interests.

Observing at City Plazas

What is the name of the plaza? Where do you see its name? How old is the plaza? Does the sign tell when it was built? Was the plaza named for a person or its location? What is the entry to the plaza like? Is there more than one entry? Are there signs at the entrance such as "No smoking" or "No animals allowed"? Is the plaza enclosed or open air? Are there grassy areas nearby? Is there a parking area nearby or underground? Do you hear music as you enter the plaza? Is there a directory showing where the group is standing? Take some time to study the map to learn the locations of different places in the plaza. Choose one or two destinations from the map and encourage the children to help you find the destination using the directions on the map.

As you walk around the plaza, notice the different types of businesses. Invite the children to call out the names of stores and what they sell, and keep a list of them. Are any areas closed off for renovation or construction? Read the signs to determine whether the previous stores have moved to new locations and what will take their place. Are there kiosks with specialty items for sale? What items are sold in the kiosks? What is the difference between a kiosk and a store?

What kinds of decorative items do you see at the plaza? Are there skylights, fountains, or potted plants? Is there artwork, such as murals or sculptures? Why are decorative items important in plazas? Are there benches for people to sit on? How many restrooms are there? Do individual stores have restrooms? Which stores do and do not have restrooms? Are there escalators, stairs, or elevators?

Take the children inside a store, if possible. If you go inside a clothing store, ask the children to look for specific things, such as interesting displays, dressing rooms, cash registers, and salespeople. What kinds of questions do shoppers ask salespeople in clothing stores? Why do stores have displays inside and in their windows? What is a mannequin? How many mannequins are in the window displays? How many are in the store? Who dresses the mannequins and when do they do it? Where do you find the price tags on clothing items? Is there music playing inside the store? Is it the same music that is playing throughout the plaza?

Are there restaurants or food courts in the plaza? What kinds of food do they sell? Are there coffee shops? Are there pet stores in the plaza? Is there an ice rink? Are there any bookstores in the plaza? Can the children think of any kinds of stores that are not in the plaza? What are they? Why aren't those kinds of stores or businesses found in plazas?

Are a lot of people shopping or eating in the plaza? What are the different kinds of jobs people have in plazas? Who cleans the plaza and takes care of the plants? Who cleans the stores?

What is the floor made of? What colors are the walls of the plaza? What colors are the walls inside stores? Do some stores have their own special way of decorating?

Categorizing and Counting
Invite the children to look for and count different things in the plaza.

- How many stores sell the same items? For example, how many stores sell clothing, shoes, or electronics? Are any stores specifically for men, women, or children?

- How many areas are there for sitting and waiting?
- How many animals are there in the plaza?
- How many steps does it take to get from one location to another location? Have children guess how many steps they will take before actually counting.
- What is the total number of businesses and stores in the plaza?
- Ask the children for ideas of other things to count. Have older children work in pairs.

Taking Photographs and Recordings
Take photographs of the different types of stores and businesses. Record some of the sounds of the plaza.

  Using the Senses

Do you hear music? Is it live? If not, where does the music come from? Do you hear water from a fountain or water display? Do you hear people talking? Close your eyes. What else do you hear?

What do you smell? Do you smell food? Do you smell perfume? Do different stores have different smells? Are there any smells you can't identify?

After the Walk

After returning to the center, revisit any lists you may have made with the children prior to the walk. Did the children see the stores or businesses they thought they would see? If children had wanted to pretend to buy items, were there stores that sold those items? Had any of the children visited the plaza before? Did they see things they hadn't noticed before? If so, what were they?

Older Children

How good are the children's memories? Working together as a group, could they create a floor plan or a mural of the plaza? If children create a floor plan, have them bring the floor plan with them the next time you visit the plaza to check the accuracy of their design.

Ask the children to consider the reasons for public artwork, such as statues and sculptures. Then invite them to pretend they have been commissioned to create a piece of artwork for the plaza. What would they create? Would it be realistic or abstract? How would they describe it to others? Would the artwork go inside or outside the plaza?

Plazas and marketplaces have been around for a very long time. Invite the children to research the history of plazas. When and where were the first marketplaces? What was their purpose? What did they contain?

Some people like plazas—or malls—and some do not. Invite the children to list the pros and cons of plazas or malls. When they are finished, have them share their lists with the other children. Do the children all agree on their assessments of plazas or malls? Do most of them like or dislike plazas or malls?

Have the children list the letters from A to Z. Tell them they have three minutes to list something for each letter of the alphabet that they saw or heard in the plaza. When the time is up, review the children's lists as a group. For example, ask what letter A words they wrote down, B words, and so on. Was there any letter children could not think of a word for?

What were the different jobs children observed people performing at the plaza? Help the children create a list of the different jobs on a sheet of chart paper. Then invite them to compose a piece of descriptive writing about a worker at the plaza. Encourage the children to include the worker's age, physical characteristics, and what the person does all day on the job. Does the worker like the job? Is there another job the person would rather have? If so, what would that be? Would the children like that person's job? Why or why not?

Younger Children

For younger children, enhance the block area with items they could use to create a plaza, such as toy people, shoe boxes to represent different stores, dollhouse furniture, plastic plants, and index cards and crayons for making signs. As they create, ask them open-ended questions to reinforce learning and new vocabulary.

Talk with the children about some of the decorative features they saw at the plaza, such as fountains or sculptures. Invite the children to create miniature sculptures or statues from playdough that could be used to decorate a plaza. When they are finished, ask them to describe what they have created to other children.

On chart paper, write a group story about the trip to the plaza. Invite each child to contribute at least one sentence describing what he or she saw or did at the plaza. Afterward, the children can illustrate the sheet of paper with things related to the plaza.

Add new words associated with the plaza to an existing word wall.

To enhance children's vocabulary, ask them to think about some of the places and things they saw at the plaza. Name a place, such as a card shop, and ask the children to name things they remember seeing or hearing in the card shop. List their suggestions on chart paper. Review the list with them afterward.

Invite the children to think of riddles related to the plaza and what they saw and did there. You could begin by saying, "I am something made from paper. I have many pages. Sometimes my pages have only words on them, and sometimes they have pictures on them. What am I?" [A book.] Work with individual children who may struggle to think of riddles by asking them to think of things they remember doing, such as riding on the escalator or listening to the water splash in the fountain.

 **Revisiting the Walk**

Visit the plaza during different seasons of the year to observe how the merchandise in some stores, such as clothing stores or housewares stores, changes according to season. Are there other reasons why stores might change their inventory, such as new products or new bestsellers?

Books

Bullard, Lisa, and Brandon Reibeling. 2003. *My neighborhood: Places and faces.* Minneapolis: Picture Window Books.

Caseley, Judith. 2002. *On the town: A community adventure.* New York: Greenwillow.

Cumpiano, Ina, and José Ramírez. 2005. *Quinito's neighborhood/El vecindario de Quinito.* San Francisco: Children's Book Press.

Harshman, Marc, and Barbara Garrison. 2007. *Only one neighborhood.* New York: Dutton Children's Books.

Holland, Gini. 2004. *I live in the city/Vivo en la ciudad.* Milwaukee, WI: Weekly Reader Early Learning Library.

Hollenbeck, Kathleen M., and Paige Billin-Frye. 1997. *Neighborhoods and communities: Activities, map & model projects, literature links.* New York: Scholastic Professional Books.

Komaiko, Leah, and Barbara Westman. 1990. *My perfect neighborhood.* New York: Harper & Row.

Maestro, Betsy, and Guillio Maestro. 1990. *Taxi: A book of city words.* New York: Clarion.

McFarlane, Sheryl, and Kim LaFave. 2003. *What's that sound? In the city.* Markham, ON: Fitzhenry & Whiteside.

Milich, Zoran. 2002. *City signs.* Toronto: Kids Can Press.

———. 2003. *The city ABC book.* Toronto: Kids Can Press.

———. 2004. *City colors.* Toronto: Kids Can Press.

Pancella, Peggy. 2006. *City.* Chicago: Heinemann Library.

Trumbauer, Lisa, and Gail Saunders-Smith. 2005. *Living in a city.* Mankato, MN: Capstone Press.

Ward, S. 2000. *I live in a city.* New York: PowerKids Press.

Hardware/Home Improvement Store Walk

Before the Walk

Some people love home improvement stores and would rather browse there than anywhere else. Those people tend to like to fix or make things. Other people never go into home improvement stores, except maybe to have keys made. Home improvement stores present wonderful learning opportunities for young children. Activities afterward can involve real supplies purchased from hardware stores that are sturdy and appeal to children. (Some children will be entertained for hours simply hammering things into blocks of wood!)

Before the walk, talk with the children about their experiences with home improvement stores. Have any children been to them? What do home improvement stores contain? What did the children do while there? What did the adult they were with purchase? Did she need items for things she was constructing or fixing? Was he buying paint or garden supplies?

On a trip to a home improvement store, children can

- see a large variety of tools in all sizes and how they are organized and displayed

- learn about all the different small items people use to fix things or hold things together

- study how this store works and what people do there

- watch keys being made

- buy things to use in many projects

- notice all the things home improvement stores sell that are used every day in our homes

Home improvement stores have many interesting items available—usually on low shelves that present enormous temptations to young children. Therefore, take only a small group of closely supervised children on this trip, and give them specific instructions about picking out things for the group to buy. For example, they can pick out a certain number of nails or screws of such and such a size. Before venturing into this type of store, children must be able to follow directions and understand which things they can touch and handle. This trip is not recommended for toddlers because too many small, dangerous objects are too accessible. If you have a toddler among older children, be sure the toddler is in a stroller or attached to you or another adult at all times.

Words to Use and Learn

aisle	hinge	nail	saw
drill	intercom	nut	screw/screwdriver
forklift	key	paint/paintbrush	tape measure
hammer	lock	power tool	tool belt
hardware	lumber	sandpaper	tools

Things to Bring on the Walk

✓ a spiral notebook that includes the children's questions and notes about experiences that might interest them (provocations), and for noting your observations of the children during the walk

✓ a camera

✓ clipboards and paper for the children

✓ writing and drawing tools

✓ shopping list and money to purchase small items for the children to explore further after the walk, such as sandpaper, nails, small tools, plastic tubing, large-size washers, nuts, and bolts

✓ measuring tools, such as tape measures, rulers, or string

✓ backpacks or paper bags for collecting free items, such as coupons, or for items you have purchased

✓ a tape recorder or other recording device

During the Walk

Consider using some of the following suggestions during the walk to help children learn about hardware or home improvement stores. Should children discover other aspects of the store that interest them, be sure to help them pursue and later document those interests.

Observing at Home Improvement Stores

Notice the general organization of the store. Point out to children the categories of items in the store, and how the things that are used for similar purposes are grouped in the same section: paint, plumbing supplies, tools, and so on.

List the different items available in the store. Call attention to items, such as doorknobs, hinges, light switches, and handles, that children may not have seen unattached. Point out light bulbs, appliance parts, hooks, trash cans, water stoppers, and other household items.

Browse one section of the store at a time, noticing the tremendous variety of hardware items and the varying sizes of those items. Ask children to name and describe the uses of as many items as they can.

Call attention to different types of hand tools, such as screwdrivers, hammers, and wrenches.

Notice how the storage space, shelves, walls, and counters are adapted to accommodate the types of items sold in the store. How are large things and small things arranged and displayed?

Point out how items are labeled. Talk about what those fractions or inch marks on the hardware items mean.

Notice the prices of various items in the store, especially the different range of prices for the same type of items.

If possible, watch specialized activities in the store such as employees operating machines to shake paint cans or make keys, or using forklifts to remove items from the top of shelves.

Watch the way employees check out customers' purchases. Do the clerks get items for customers, or do customers help themselves and take them to a central check-out?

Notice seasonal items the store may carry. Notice large equipment the store has available for rent, such as floor polishers, rug cleaners, and tillers. Talk about what each machine does and how much it costs to rent. Does the store rent many things? Talk about why people rent these things.

Counting Items

Count the different sizes of the same type of item. How many sizes of nails, washers, and screws are there? How many different sizes of screwdrivers, hammers, and paintbrushes?

Measure several items and match the measurements to the store's signs.

Count the different brands of the same item, such as paint, mops, toasters, and irons.

Call attention to container sizes, such as gallons, half-gallons, and quarts of paint, and other liquid items.

Measure some tools to note differences in the size of things, such as the heads of hammers, blades of saws, and length of screwdrivers.

Compare the long- and short-handled versions of tools and cleaning implements. Talk about all the uses of these items.

   Using the Senses

Feel the variety of textures of items, such as the different kinds of sandpaper, ridges on screws, bristles of brushes, rollers from mops, and smooth metals of items.

Notice the shades of colors of paint and on paint charts.

Listen to the sounds of the hardware store. Do you hear grinding or cutting sounds or noises from moving heavy equipment?

Are there particular smells in the store, such as smells related to oiling machines or from paint or cleaning items or from bags of things sold in the store?

Wondering about Home Improvement Stores

Ask the children to guess the uses of some of the more familiar items, but ones they may not have noticed before. Guess what some of the unfamiliar items might be used for.

Think about what the store does with seasonal things it doesn't sell.

If the store sells toys, wonder why it does.

What would happen if the store didn't have separate spaces for all the small hardware items?

Think about how the store got its name.

Purchasing Items

Buy different kinds of sandpaper to sand blocks or make sandpaper letters.

Buy large nails and small tools to use at the workbench. Buy plastic tubing and large-sized washers to make stringing toys.

Buy large nuts and bolts and plumbing joints to use for fit-together games.

? Ask the owner or clerk how they keep track of everything in the store. How do they know when they need to order more items?

? Does the store sell other things you can't see, such as items from a catalog?

? How do they decide what things to sell and where do they get them?

? How do they decide what something should cost or what things to put on sale for a special price?

Ask for or collect paint sample color cards to use later.

After the Walk

Talk about the walk and write down the children's impressions of the home improvement store.

Look at hinges on cupboards and doors and talk about how they work. Look for other items in your room that you saw in the store (such as light switches and cupboard handles) and call attention to how they are used. Look inside closets and hidden spots for other things you saw, such as cleaning supplies, tools, and hooks. Make up lists of things you find, the rooms they are in, and their uses.

Look at plumbing and other pipes and talk about their uses. Notice faucets and other such items. Make up some generalizations about the hardware store and its importance and usefulness.

Older Children

Invite children to help set up a workshop using the items purchased at the home improvement store. Brainstorm a list of items that should go in a workshop. Organize a workbench area using different-colored cans or boxes for different-sized nails, screws, washers, and so on. Invite children to draw outlines of tools.

Obtain scrap lumber, and let the children pound nails to make simple objects. Use soft lumber or acoustical tile so the children can pound the nails easily. Closely supervise children when they use tools.

Children can establish a fix-it area. Bring in real tools and materials to use, and set up a fix-it corner to repair toys. Children can sand blocks, form puzzle pieces from wood, replace hinges, and tighten loose screws. Talk about the idea of recycling, that is, fixing things instead of throwing them away.

Working together as a group, have the children create a list of all the things they saw in the home improvement store. Children may not know the names of some of the items they saw. If so, have children describe the items and work with them to discover their names. This list may be very long and the activity may last several days, which will help children recognize the large variety of objects in home improvement stores and why these stores must be so well organized.

Invite the children to write "user manuals" for some of the items they saw at the store, such as sandpaper, black and white pipes, and electrical wire. Have children name the items and briefly describe what the items are used for and how to use them.

Were there items the children did not see in the home improvement store? What were the items and why weren't they in the store? This activity may be more challenging if completed after the children have created a list of all the things they saw in the home improvement store.

Have the children use the list they created of all the things found in a home improvement store to create a Home Improvement Store Dictionary, complete with definitions.

Younger Children

Younger children in particular will spend a lot of time in a workshop area where they are allowed to pound and saw things. Consider how they can be involved in setting up the workshop.

Introduce materials purchased at the store to other areas in the room, such as sandpaper in the blocks area or small items in the art center for children to use with playdough to create nuts-and-bolts people or wire people. Many of the items from the store could also be added to the dramatic play area to create a home improvement store.

Have children help create a list on chart paper of all the things they saw in the home improvement store.

Work with the children to create tool puppets from small paper bags, such as saws, hammers, nails, power tools, and paint cans. Then have them imagine that the tools talk to each when the store is closed at night. What might a nail say to a hammer? What might a bag of cement say to an ax? What might the keys talk about among themselves?

Show the children four or five different grades of sandpaper. Explain that sandpaper is identified by grade, or by number, from most fine to most coarse. Instead of using numbers to identify the different types of sandpaper, what words would children use to describe them? What are the finest grades called? "Slightly scratchy" to "More scratchy"? What about the coarsest grades?

Make sandpaper letters with different grades of sandpaper that children can use to create rubbings. After children are no longer interested in making rubbings, create a sandpaper alphabet display on a wall or bulletin board.

Revisiting the Walk

Next time you visit a home improvement store with the children, arrange to meet with a store employee beforehand, either someone who could give the children a more personal tour of the store or someone who is a specialist in a particular area, such as electrical or paint.

Books

Archer, Amanda, and Deborah van de Leijgraaf. 2006. *My dad's toolbox.* Hauppauge, NY: Barron's Educational Series, Inc.

Auch, Alison. 2003. *Garden tools.* Minneapolis: Compass Point Books.

Dahl, Michael. 1996. *Wheels and axles.* Mankato, MN: Bridgestone Books.

Dahl, Michael, and Denise Shea. 2006. *Pull, lift, and lower: A book about pulleys.* Minneapolis: Picture Window Books.

Disney Press (Firm). 2008. *Manny's book of tools: An interactive book.* New York: Disney Press.

Fowler, Allan. 1995. *What magnets can do.* New York: Children's Press.

———. 2001. *Simple machines.* New York: Children's Press.

Gibbons, Gail. 1982. *Tool book.* New York: Holiday House.

Glover, David. 1997. *Screws.* Crystal Lake, IL: Rigby Interactive Library.

Kelley, True. 1994. *Hammers and mops, pencils and pots: A first book of tools and gadgets we use around the house.* New York: Crown Publishers.

Miura, Taro. 2006. *Tools.* San Francisco: Chronicle Books.

Newhouse, Maxwell. 2008. *The house that Max built.* Toronto: Tundra Books.

Oxlade, Chris. 2007. *Screws.* North Mankato, MN: Smart Apple Media.

Simon, Charnan, and Robert Squier. 2007. *Uncle Jack is a carpenter.* Chanhassen, MN: Child's World.

Sturges, Philemon, and Shari Halpern. 2006. *I love tools!* New York: HarperCollins.

Market/Grocery Store Walk

Before the Walk

Most children have been to a grocery store or market many times—but the trips were probably rushed events, not educational experiences. However, grocery stores and markets are literally stocked with wonderful learning opportunities for children to practice categorization skills, observe and learn about likenesses and differences among similar things, and see multiple versions of the same thing (for example, fruits and vegetables that are whole or cut up in various ways, canned, dried, or frozen). Trips to grocery stores and markets also offer opportunities to

- **observe what people who work in grocery stores and markets do**

- **learn how grocery stores function and how foods are packaged and items are arranged for display**

- **study and discuss nutrition concepts**

- **discover the different departments and what types of things are in each one**

- **consider the prices of different food items and the concept of budgeting**

- **find out where different foods come from**

- **talk about environmentally friendly concepts related to food shopping, such as buying locally produced foods, selecting foods with minimal packaging, and reusing paper bags or using cloth bags brought from home**

Many large grocery stores offer tours for groups of children, but there are also many things to see and explore on your own. Before visiting the store with children, spend some time in the store taking notes about things that might interest your particular group. Also keep in mind that because the learning opportunities in grocery stores are so rich, you may want to make multiple trips, each time focusing on a different learning objective as well as reinforcing previous concepts.

Prior to the walk, talk with the children about their experiences with grocery stores and markets. Do they go to the grocery store with their families? How often? Which stores or markets have they been to? Ask the children to describe the stores and markets. Find out whether the store you visit is similar to or different from the ones they describe. Do the children have any questions about grocery stores, such as what the people who work there do? How are markets different from grocery stores? What do markets sell? Are markets open year-round? Write down the things the children tell you about grocery stores and markets as well as any questions they might have.

Words to Use and Learn

aisle	cash register	counters	frozen food
bar code	check-out counter	coupon	manager
bulk foods	check-out lanes	dairy	produce
butcher	condiments	delicatessen	receipt
cashier	conveyor belt	farmer	scale

Things to Bring on the Walk

✓ a spiral notebook that includes the children's questions and notes about experiences that might interest them (provocations), and for noting your observations of the children during the walk

✓ a camera

✓ notebooks for the children

✓ writing and drawing tools

✓ a tape recorder or other recording device

✓ backpacks or paper bags for collecting things or carrying purchases

✓ measuring tools, such as tape measures, rulers, or string

During the Walk

Consider using some of the following suggestions during the walk to help children learn about grocery stores and markets. Should children discover other aspects of the store that interest them, be sure to help them pursue and later document those interests.

Observing at Markets/Grocery Stores

Notice the general appearance of the building as you approach. Is it small or large, new or old, busy or quiet? How many times does the store's name appear in front of or on the store itself? What features around the building are part of the store's operation, such as an area for deliveries, a grocery pickup or drive-through area, areas for grocery carts, or areas for recycling bottles or other items? Is there advertising on the windows or in other places around the store? Observe people delivering products to the store. How are the products unloaded and moved into the store? Notice the loading docks around the side or back of the store and point out that the height of the docks is the same height as trucks.

Notice the entryway to the store. Are there double doors, automatic doors, or separate entrances and exits? Is there a bulletin board with notices or other items on display to catch people's attention? Are there free coupons or information about store specials or sales?

Look at the store's arrangement as you walk in and notice the different sections and the check-out area. How much can you see from the store's entrance? How are the aisles labeled—with numbers, words, or both? Talk about how different areas are grouped and read signs that tell what is in each area, such as meat, produce, or baked goods. Is there a pharmacy or floral department?

Observe check-out procedures. How many counters are there? How do people know which check-out to go to? Are there lines of shoppers? Are there any express lanes? What is the item limit in the express lane? Notice the equipment in use. Are there conveyor belts, computerized cash registers, scanners, or any other special equipment? Watch the cashier and the people bagging groceries. Do the cashiers bag the groceries or are there people at the end of the counter whose job it is to bag groceries? Do they follow any system in doing their jobs? Do shoppers bag their own groceries? Do baggers set aside certain items to bag last? Which items do they set aside? Why? What happens when an item doesn't have a price on it? Do some people have their own grocery bags they brought from home? How can you tell? Why do shoppers bring their own bags? Do people carry out their own groceries? Do baggers accompany shoppers to their cars to help load their groceries?

Explore a few sections of the store, such as the produce department and the meat department. Point out and name items or ask the children to name different items. Notice how things are displayed with the same type of items grouped together. Are like items displayed in the same way? For example, in the produce department, do the tips of the carrots all point in the same direction? Are all of the apples stacked the same way? Why might this be so? Talk about categories or groupings and different ways of packaging the same items, such as cans or boxes of soup and bags or cans of coffee. Do all of the labels face the same direction? Why? How are the display racks, counters, shelves, and bins especially suited to the items they contain? Look at the many different types of the same things: different types of apples, lettuces, meats, canned beans, packages of pasta, yogurts, and cereals.

Notice how items are packaged and marked. Call attention to how things are sold and priced. Is it by the item or by the pound? How can people decide what is a good buy? Look for signs that give price information and tell the children what different things cost. Does the store have its own brand? If so, what kinds of items carry the store's brand? What are expiration dates? Why are expiration dates important? Do all food items have expiration dates? Why or why not? What kind of information is included on nutrition labels? How important are nutrition labels? Are there sections for bulk food? Explain bulk foods to children and how price is determined. Notice the kinds of food items in the bulk-foods section as well as the bags and labels people use to identify items and their prices. Compare the price of bulk items such as cereals and nuts to the price of cereals and nuts that are already packaged.

Notice the jobs people do at the store. Do people have special tasks? Do employees wear special uniforms or name tags? Do their name tags indicate what their jobs are in the store? Do some employees wear hairnets or gloves? In which departments do those people work? Do you see employees marking items for sale, stocking shelves or freezers, or replacing produce in the produce section? Is anyone giving out free samples of food? What type of food is it? Talk about why some stores give out samples to taste. Is anyone

cleaning up spills? How might the spill have happened? How many employees do you see in all?

Notice some of the specialized sections the store may have, such as diet foods, ethnic foods, and natural foods. What are diet foods, ethnic foods, and natural foods? Talk about the large areas for frozen foods or baked goods. Notice the difference in display cases. Which areas of the store are the largest? Which are the smallest?

How many shoppers are in the store? Are they all pushing carts? Are any children riding in the carts? Are some shoppers carrying baskets?

Counting and Comparing

There are so many things to count in a grocery store or market! Depending on the ages of the children in your group, here are a few things they might have fun counting:

- the number of aisles, check-out counters, wheels on the carts, people working in each area
- the number of different types of the same thing, such as different kinds of apples, squash, ice cream, yogurt, cereal, beans, juice, chips, or tea
- the different-size containers of milk and other dairy products, and the amount in each container, such as pint, quart, half-gallon, and gallon
- the number of shoppers in different check-out lanes

Shopping on a Budget

For older children, give them clipboards and pencils, and tell them to put together healthy meals for breakfast, lunch, and dinner on a budget. Have children work in small groups so that an adult can be with each group as they walk around the store. Assign a dollar amount to each meal, for example, under five dollars for breakfast, under eight dollars for lunch, and under twelve dollars for dinner. Make sure children list the items and their prices. Discuss the children's meals and prices when you return from the walk.

👂 👃 Using the Senses

Have children stand in different sections of the store, close their eyes, and listen. Stores are such visually stimulating places, it may be necessary to close off one sense to really use another. Do they hear items being scanned, carts slamming or moving, voices or music on the intercom, phones ringing, babies crying, people talking? List all of the sounds the children mention.

What smells do they notice in the store? Move around to different sections. Can they smell coffee beans grinding, bread baking, or chicken roasting in the deli? Are there identifiable smells in the fish department or produce section? Sniff particular items, such as onions, herbs, or garlic, and talk about strong smells. Are employees giving out food samples that children can smell?

Wondering about Markets/Grocery Stores

Why are there so many different brands of items?

Think about why some areas of the store have equipment to keep things cold. How is that done? Why is it done?

What happens to the baked goods that don't get sold each day? Think about the differences between baked goods in boxes and fresh baked goods. Why can one be kept for several days while others have to be sold each day? What happens to produce or meat that isn't sold by a particular date?

How long does it take different food items to reach the grocery store after they are grown or packaged? Which food items do the children think came from your area? Which came from out of state? Which came from out of the country? Look at the labels on various items in the produce department to see how many were grown locally and how many were grown elsewhere. Which produce item traveled the farthest to reach the store?

What would it be like to work in a grocery store? Do grocery store employees get their food for free? Talk about employee discounts with the children.

Collecting Items

Ask store managers for pictures of foods, old displays, or other throwaways that might be useful to the children, such as in a dramatic play area or in the block area.

Taking Photographs and Recordings

Ask the store manager for permission to take photographs or make recordings. Take photographs of the store and the children involved in various activities, such as listening to an employee give a store tour. Record the employee giving a tour or record casual conversations with the children as you walk through the store.

Asking Questions

Children may be curious about answers to the following questions:

? Ask a department manager to show you the back-room work areas where items are received, wrapped, or sorted. Is there an area where returned bottles and cans are kept?

? Ask to see special equipment employees use for packaging or marking products and items. Have an employee demonstrate the equipment for the children.

? Ask to see the bakery kitchen or receiving area, if there is one. Notice the huge pans and storage racks for holding baked goods. If the store does baking on the premises, look at the huge mixers, pans, and ovens. If there is a cake decorator at work, ask for a demonstration.

? Ask to see the employee break room and time clock.

 ## After the Walk

Talk about the trip and ask the children what they remember about the store. How does the store you visited compare to ones they have been to before? Discuss with the children things they may have looked for in the store or questions they had about the store prior to the walk. Did they see things in the store they never noticed in other grocery stores? What did they learn about grocery stores that they didn't know before?

Where else do people shop for food? Talk about stores that have foods from other cultures. Mention farmers' markets, which have things from local farms or special shops, such as bakeries, coffee shops, and co-ops.

Show children the photographs from the walk. Consider making a display of the photographs and using them to talk about nutrition concepts.

Ask the children if they still have questions about grocery stores or markets. Make a list of things they are still curious about related to grocery stores or things they saw in the store. Find out the answers. Or plan another trip back to the store to find the answers.

Older Children

Did any of the older children pretend to shop for healthy meals on a budget? Invite them to share their healthy meals with others. Was it easy or difficult to stay within the budget? Why or why not?

Produce displays in grocery stores and markets are very colorful and include many different shapes. Some children may want to paint pictures of produce displays or sculpt displays from different-colored playdough or clay. Talk with the children about how fruits and vegetables have been the subject of artistic works for a long time. Show children examples of still-life and cubist paintings. Bring in real fruit or vegetables for children to use as models for their artwork.

What happens after grocery stores close up at night? Invite the children to create stories or puppet shows involving happenings in a grocery store after hours, such as all of the produce items coming to life and carrying on conversations. What would produce items have to talk about? How would their voices sound? What would happen if an employee accidentally heard them talking?

Have children research the MyPyramid food guidance system and create a large-scale food pyramid on a wall or bulletin board; see www.mypyramid.gov for information. Children can use pictures of food collected at the grocery store or cutouts from magazines to attach to the food groups on the food pyramid display. Ask the children to share what they learned about nutrition with the younger children.

Invite the children to gather favorite family recipes. Bring in your own favorite recipes and create a class cookbook of favorite recipes. These might also make nice gifts for families.

As a group, create a list on chart paper of all the words children can think of related to grocery stores and markets. How many words did they come up with? Then challenge the children to write stories about a trip to a grocery store or describe the visit while using as many words as they can from the list. Have children share their writing when they are finished. Did anyone use all of the words on the list?

Younger Children

After discussing the walk with younger children, ask them to consider what kinds of things they would need to set up a grocery store in the dramatic play area. Make a list of the children's suggestions on chart paper. Have the children bring in empty boxes, cans, and other food packages. Help the children sort the items on shelves and mark prices on them. (Cut out grocery ads from the newspaper or use the flyers and coupons collected from the store to get an idea of prices.) Ask the children whether they can find ads for any of the items for which you have empty packages. The children can decide on specials for the day and so forth.

Create a store bulletin board by dividing a bulletin board into areas and using corrugated strips of paper to represent shelves within each area. Put names over each area to correspond to the areas you saw in the store: bakery, produce, meat department, and so on. Cut out pictures of store items from magazine ads or use the ads and flyers collected from the store. Let the children attach them to the bulletin board in the proper sections. Encourage the children to organize the items on the shelves as they were in the store.

Add new words related to grocery stores, markets, and food to an existing word wall or create a word wall dedicated to grocery stores, food, and nutrition.

Use your local bookstore or library to collect a variety of books about food and markets around the world. Ask the children to think about how the foods are different or the same as the foods they eat. Are there any foods they learned about in the books they would like to try? Visit local stores that sell some of these foods and bring them in for the children to taste and discuss.

Is there a snack food for each letter of the alphabet? With the children, create a list of snack foods from A to Z. Each day, serve a snack whose name begins with a different letter of the alphabet. Keep a list of the snack foods you have enjoyed. Consider posting the list in the grocery store in the dramatic play area.

Revisiting the Walk

Grocery stores and markets are rich with learning opportunities for children. Revisit the store several times throughout the year, each time looking for different things or engaging the children in different activities. Have the children pay attention to the different fruits and vegetables offered in the produce section according to each new season.

Books

Canizares, Susan, Kama Einhorn, James Williamson, and Alex Ostroy. 2002. *Supermarket.* New York: Scholastic.

Flanagan, Alice K., and Christine Osinski. 1996. *A busy day at Mr. Kang's grocery store.* New York: Children's Press.

Gallacher, Lorraine, Bill Cosby, and Jane Howell. 2001. *Let's go to the supermarket!* New York: Simon Spotlight/Nick Jr.

Greene, Carol. 1999. *Grocers sell us food.* Chanhassen, MN: Child's World.

Hautzig, David. 1994. *At the supermarket.* New York: Orchard Books.

Hill, Mary. 2003. *Signs at the store. Signs in my world.* New York: Children's Press.

Hoena, B. A. 2004. *The supermarket.* Pebble plus. Mankato, MN: Capstone Press.

Johnston, Marianne. 2000. *Let's visit the supermarket.* New York: Rosen Pub.

Krull, Kathleen, and Melanie Hope Greenberg. 2001. *Supermarket.* New York: Holiday House.

Leeper, Angela. 2004. *Grocery store. Field trip!* Chicago: Heinemann Library.

Lewin, Ted. 2006. *How much? Visiting markets around the world.* New York: HarperCollins.

Mayer, Cassie. 2007. *Markets. Our global community.* Chicago: Heinemann Library.

Pan, Hui-Mei. 2004. *What's in grandma's grocery bag?* New York: Star Bright Books.

Ripley, Catherine, and Scot Ritchie. 1995. *Do the doors open by magic? And other supermarket questions.* Toronto: Owl Books.

Schaefer, Lola M. 2000. *Supermarket.* Chicago: Heinemann Library.

Vehicles Walk

Before the Walk

Moving vehicles, such as trucks, semis, moving vans, cars, buses, taxicabs, and motorcycles, hold endless fascination for younger children—the huge number of books and materials on this subject and the large truck and vehicle sections of toy stores confirm this notion. Walks focusing on vehicles capitalize on that interest and help children become observant learners. There are also many educational opportunities for older children during walks that focus on vehicles. For example, older children can be encouraged to think about how vehicles affect the environment and how people can work together to reduce the number of vehicles on the road each day.

On a vehicles walk, you can encourage children to

🔍 **observe different kinds of vehicles and think about the work they do**

🔍 **notice characteristics of vehicles and learn about their various parts**

🔍 **learn how vehicles are driven and about safety around vehicles**

🔍 **compare different types of vehicles and think about the roles they play in the transportation system**

For younger children, display picture books about vehicles along with model or toy vehicles. Ask the children how vehicles are different from one another. For example, how is a car different from a truck? How is a sports car different from a motorcycle?

Words to Use and Learn

ambulance	fire truck	motorcycle	semitrailer
bus	gasoline	pickup truck	station wagon
convertible	limousine/limo	police car	taxicab
delivery truck	mail truck	sanitation truck	tow truck
dump truck	minivan	sedan	wheel

Things to Bring on the Walk

✔ a spiral notebook that includes the children's questions and notes about experiences that might interest them (provocations), and for noting your observations of the children during the walk

✔ a camera

✔ clipboards and paper for the children

✔ writing and drawing tools

✔ picture books about trucks and their parts

✔ a tape recorder or other recording device

During the Walk

Consider using some of the following suggestions during the walk to help children learn about vehicles. Should children discover other aspects of vehicles that interest them, be sure to help them pursue and later document those interests.

Identifying Vehicles

Find a parked truck and examine it, noticing the way it is put together. Take along a picture book with names and pictures of the parts of trucks. Identify the parts and compare the pictures to the real thing.

Make a list of all the different vehicles you see. Notice the colors of the vehicles as well. Make notes of vehicles the children are most familiar with and the ones they want to learn more about. Older children can keep track of the different vehicles and their colors to review later.

Comparing Vehicles

Count the number of wheels on different vehicles. Are the tires the same size on all vehicles? Do the vehicles all have the same number of tires?

Compare cars and trucks. In what ways are they alike and how are they different? Look for specific parts that each might have. Notice their similarities and differences, such as mirrors, windows, seats, tires, and license plates.

Listen to the sounds different vehicles make as they go by. Compare the sounds of trucks and cars. What can you tell from the sounds? Challenge the children to hold still and close their eyes. Can they identify different vehicles with their eyes closed?

Observing Vehicles

Notice how different vehicles are driven. Where does the driver sit? Are there differences in where the driver sits in a car compared to other vehicles (such as buses, large trucks, vans, or mail delivery trucks)? Where do the passengers sit? How many passengers can different types of vehicles carry? Do any vehicles have car seats? Where are the car seats located?

Wondering about Vehicles

Wonder what type of loads the trucks are carrying. What clues do the children have about what work the truck does? How is the truck suited to the work it does? What parts does it need for its job? Could a mail delivery truck tow a car?

How might it feel to drive different vehicles? How might driving a truck feel different from driving a motorcycle or a bus? Which vehicles go the fastest? Which vehicles go the slowest?

Can vehicles go backward? How do drivers see when they back up? What happens when trucks that have trailers need to go backward? Do the children hear a ringing noise like a bell or loud beep made by some trucks when they begin to go in reverse? What does the sound mean?

Where do large trucks get gas? Can large trucks use regular gas stations?

Think about why some vehicles have more wheels than others.

Wonder if anyone can drive all types of vehicles. Do drivers need to know about special things when driving certain vehicles? Do drivers have to pass certain tests to be able to drive certain vehicles?

Why do all vehicles have license plates? What do license plates look like? Do they all have the same number of letters and numerals on them? Why are the names of states on license plates? Older children might enjoy keeping track of the number of out-of-state license plates they see on vehicles.

Some Safety Notes

In looking for vehicles to observe, keep the children's safety in mind. If you are watching for vehicles near a busy street, be sure all children are far away from the street and intersections. In looking at parked vehicles, be sure the children stand at a safe distance from the street and a safe distance from any possible moving vehicles, such as a vehicle about to park or pull out of a parking spot.

The safest spots for vehicle watching are on your own center or school grounds. Watch for vehicles driving by or visit one parked on your street or in a nearby parking area. Try to time your observation to take advantage of vehicles visiting your immediate area rather than venturing into busy places that may present safety problems.

After the Walk

Talk about the walk and write down the children's observations. What general statements about vehicles can the children make? Here are some samples:

- Large trucks have many more wheels than cars.
- Trucks that carry heavy loads need more wheels.
- Some vehicles carry a lot more people than others.
- To operate certain vehicles, you need special driver's licenses.
- Truck drivers need to sit up high to see the road well and judge distances.
- Vehicles such as sports cars and motorcycles go a lot faster than buses and big trucks.

Questions you ask might help the children think of these and other statements. Try to get the children to tell some general things they have noticed about vehicles.

Discuss the ways people use vehicles, and set up a transportation bulletin board showing different kinds of vehicles and what they're used for. Mention the products some trucks carry and the places they take those products (for example, a trailer taking cars to a car dealership or a mail truck delivering the mail to people's homes). With older children, discuss the role of vehicles as part of the transportation system. How do people transport big items (such as furniture and refrigerators) from stores to homes, or from their old house to a new house when they move? Who determines bus routes? How are traffic lights controlled and by whom? Where are school buses kept at night? How do farmers get the things they grow to the market? What things do trucks carry from factory to store? How do vans get turned into ambulances?

Older Children

Suggest that older children make models of their favorite vehicles. Invite the children to suggest materials to use to make their models. Materials might include shoe boxes, scrap wood, or even wire.

Bring in a large appliance box and have a group of older children work to turn the box into a specific type of vehicle, such as an ambulance or sports car. Encourage the children to look at pictures of the real vehicles, both the exterior and the interior, to help them make the vehicle as realistic as possible. The children could also use the box to invent their own special vehicle.

Do the children know how long it takes to manufacture the average car? Have the children research car manufacturing and make books showing how cars are made, from design to showroom floor.

If the children could be any kind of vehicle, what would they be? Invite the children to write their own books called "If I Were a Vehicle, I Would Be a . . ."

Encourage the children to create acrostic poems about vehicles. Acrostic poems begin with a word such as *Zipcar* or *ambulance* written vertically on a sheet of paper. Each letter of the word starts a new sentence or phrase that is related to the word.

For example, using the word *truck*, an acrostic poem might look like this:

TRUCK

Tons of metal
Rolling along
Under and over bridges
Carrying
Kilos of stuff everywhere.

Challenge the children to think about solutions to some of the problems caused by vehicles such as air pollution. What can people do instead of driving their cars? What kinds of cars should people be driving to limit air pollution? What will happen if the world runs out of the oil that is needed to operate all our vehicles? Encourage children to write their thoughts in a letter format to an environmental group or local politician.

Younger Children

For younger children, suggest they make a large mural of all the different vehicles they saw during the walk. Place a large sheet of paper on the floor. Place the materials children will need nearby, such as magazines, glue, scissors, and drawing tools. Children can cut out pictures of vehicles from the magazines to glue to the mural and draw on the mural using crayon or markers.

Bring in a large appliance box and invite the children to help turn the box into a vehicle they can play in.

Make a big book of vehicles using magazine pictures. Work with the children to help them label the different vehicles and their parts. Ask children what other things they would like to share about vehicles and write what they say in the book. When the book is finished, display it in the group's library for the children to read.

Sing songs or perform fingerplays about vehicles. Children can use toy vehicles as props. You can download fingerplays from the Redleaf Web site, www.redleafpress.org. Enter "Hey Kids!" into the search field and follow the links.

Invite children to write poems about vehicles. To get them started, invite them to tell you what they know about certain vehicles. Then begin the poems with "Big, red fire trucks blast horns . . ." or "I wish I could drive a . . .," for example.

Add new words related to vehicles to an existing word wall or create a new word wall for vehicle-related words.

Revisiting the Walk

Next time you take the children on a vehicles walk, invite them to look for specific things. For example, they might look only for trucks or cars that are red. Or try varying the time of your walk to see whether there are more vehicles on the roads during certain times of the day. Keep track of the children's findings in a notebook or invite an older child to write things down.

Books

Coffelt, Nancy. 2006. *Pug in a truck*. Boston: Houghton Mifflin.

Delafosse, Claude, and Sophie Kniffke. 1996. *Cars and trucks and other vehicles*. A first discovery book. New York: Scholastic.

Freeman, Marcia S. 1999. *Police cars*. Mankato, MN: Pebble Books.

Kilby, Don. 2004. *Wheels at work in the city*. Toronto: Kids Can Press.

———. 2004. *Wheels at work in the country*. Toronto: Kids Can Press.

Maestro, Betsy, and Giulio Maestro. 1981. *Traffic: A book of opposites*. New York: Crown Publishers.

Ready, Dee. 1998. *Trucks*. Mankato, MN: Bridgestone Books.

Rockwell, Anne F. 2006. *Big wheels*. New York: Walker & Co.

Rockwell, Anne F., and Melanie Hope Greenberg. 2005. *Good morning, Digger*. New York: Viking.

Rotner, Shelley. 1995. *Wheels around*. Boston: Houghton Mifflin.

Royston, Angela. 1991. *Cars*. London: Dorling Kindersley.

Royston, Angela, Tim Ridley, Jane Cradock-Watson, and Dave Hopkins. 1991. *Diggers and dump trucks*. Eye openers. New York: Aladdin Books.

Schaefer, Lola M. 2000. *Tow trucks*. The transportation library. Mankato, MN: Bridgestone Books.

Stille, Darlene R. 1997. *Trucks*. A true book. New York: Children's Press.

Werther, Scott P. 2002. *Big rigs*. Reading power. New York: PowerKids Press.

Construction Site Walk

Before the Walk

Construction sites and machinery are particularly fascinating for children. Watching a building go up—from excavating the foundation to raising the roof beams—is an amazing process and one that will easily spill over into the children's play experiences and conversations. The most challenging aspect of the walk will be finding the best vantage points for children to observe things without being in the way or in any danger. Sometimes a neighboring driveway or a spot across the street will work out well for viewing the action.

Although most children have seen construction sites and construction machinery, reading a few books related to building and construction sites beforehand might stimulate the children's interest and generate a list of things to look for during the walk.

Children may also have questions that could be posed to workers at the site, such as asking the names of unfamiliar machinery, how long it will take to complete the project, and how people

learn to operate certain types of machinery. Frequent visits to a construction site offer children an ideal opportunity to

- **observe firsthand each step in the building process**

- **see how a large number of machines work and the kinds of things they can do**

- **learn about the work of the various people involved in the construction process and how they work together**

- **study the materials used in the process and how they are put together**

- **consider what can cause problems for the construction project**

- **wonder about the effects new structures have on the neighborhood, such as increased vehicle traffic, and on the natural environment, such as wild animals losing their homes**

Words to Use and Learn

backhoe	bulldozer	ducts	girder
basement	cement	dump truck	hard hat
blueprints	concrete block	excavate	pipe
brick	crane	foundation	power shovel
builder	digging	framing	rafters

Things to Bring on the Walk

✓ a spiral notebook that includes the children's questions and notes about experiences that might interest them (provocations), and for noting your observations of the children during the walk

✓ a camera

✓ clipboards and paper for the children

✓ writing and drawing tools

✓ measuring tools, such as tape measures, rulers, or string

✓ a tape recorder or other recording device

✓ backpacks or paper bags for collecting things

During the Walk

Consider using some of the following suggestions during the walk to help children learn about construction sites. Should children discover other aspects of construction that interest them, be sure to help them pursue and later document those interests.

Observing at Construction Sites

Notice the collection of machinery and materials assembled at the site. Are they arranged in a particular way? Who seems to be telling people where to put things and what to do?

Watch machines being used, such as bulldozers, power shovels, dump trucks, and cement mixers. Stay well out of the way of machines in use, but find a spot where you can see them work. Talk about how the machines move and who operates them. When machines are parked and not in use, it may be possible to observe them more closely to see how they work. Notice, for instance, that many machines have special parts, like a bulldozer blade or a crane attached to a tractor.

Try to observe various phases of construction, such as workers pouring cement for a foundation, framing the building, raising the roof beams and rafters, grading and finishing the yard, connecting the wiring, laying the pipes, and adding floors to apartment buildings.

If possible, observe the different ways workers use cranes. For tall buildings, workers often use them to deliver materials to places where they are needed. What precautions do workers in high places take, such as wearing safety harnesses or

standing on scaffolding? Notice hooks, magnets, and all other types of parts added to cranes to aid in this process.

Notice special ways the work site is prepared. Are there temporary structures on the grounds for the workers to use? Is the area fenced off? Were buildings demolished to make way for the new construction? Were tress cut down or fields plowed over?

Observe the debris and trash that accumulates as work progresses. Is it hauled away? Does there appear to be an area set aside for recyclable or reusable materials?

Observe the work various people do. Notice how the people work as a team to get tasks done. Do they give directions to each other?

Do the workers wear special clothes? Do they use anything to protect their heads, eyes, ears, or backs?

Notice hand tools or power tools in use in addition to the larger machines. If power tools are in use, where does the power come from?

Be sure to take photos of various machines and vehicles as well as the building in its current state. Record some of the sounds at the construction site. Does all of the machinery sound the same? Encourage older children to take notes about some of the things they see or make sketches of the site. Younger children can draw pictures of the site, the machines, and the workers.

Wondering about Construction Sites

Can you tell what kind of building or structure is being built? Try to guess what it might be, based on location and what you have observed so far. Does it look like any other building you have seen? Fast food restaurants tend to look alike as they go up, but they often put up signs in advance, so there's not much left to imagine. Let the children guess anyway, as it is fun to make up ideas about the building and its use.

Wonder how much it is costing to build the building. Perhaps you can get some estimates from the builders.

Think about what would look nice around the building when it is finished.

Asking Questions

? If possible, ask someone to show you specific machines and tell you about them. Be sure to consult with the general contractor about suitable times to ask questions. For example, there are times when workers are waiting for something or taking a break and can answer questions without interrupting their work.

? If appropriate, ask how workers avoid having a power shovel get stuck in the bottom of the hole it digs for the foundation.

? If someone is mixing cement, ask how it's made. Observe how it comes out of the mixer and how it is transported. Ask how long it takes to harden and how quickly the person has to work. Are there different cement types or consistencies used or is all cement the same?

? Tell the children as many of the names of machines and materials as you can. Ask someone to tell you the names of those items you don't know. Ask how people learn to operate certain types of machinery. Do they have to go to special schools or take special tests? Ask someone to show you the plans for the building. Do people keep consulting those plans?

? What happens during bad weather? Does the construction continue? What type of weather might prevent the work from being done?

Counting and Measuring

There are many things to count and measure at a construction site, including

- the number of people working, the number of trucks or machines you see, the stacks of materials, bags of cement, and other visible items

- the features you can see related to the building, such as the number of openings for windows or doors, floors, roof beams, and corner posts
- the number of trips the dump truck makes, or the number of times the cement mixer is loaded
- how long each batch of cement is mixed or how long other specific tasks take

 **After the Walk**

Talk with the children about all the things you saw on the walk. Ask what interested them the most about the site and the activities they observed. Did they learn anything about construction they didn't know before? Which jobs would the children most enjoy doing? Which jobs seem the hardest or easiest? Why? Play back any recordings you made of the various sounds at the construction site. Have the children guess what type of vehicle or machinery made the sound.

Older Children

Challenge older children to think about the word *progress* and what it means to people and the environment. Is progress a good thing? Why or why not? What might some negative aspects of progress be? For example, what happens to wild creatures, such as birds, if trees are cut down? What happens to the animals in a field when the field is paved over?

For children who are interested in building things, be sure to have a variety of materials and supplies on hand for them to work with, such as wood scraps and woodworking tools, hammers, and

wood glue. Or invite the children to paint a mural on large sheets of paper showing the progress of the building or structure they observed.

Invite older children to keep a "construction journal." Each time they visit the site, have them record the progress and draw pictures of what is new at the site.

Encourage the children to write their thoughts or concerns about progress in their construction journals. How will the new building or structure affect the community? Will there be more traffic or less traffic after the structure is built?

Invite the children to research the history of different construction vehicles and equipment, such as the dump truck, cement truck, or front-end loader. How were the various construction tasks accomplished before our modern-day construction vehicles and machinery were invented? About how much do the different machines cost?

With the children, make a list of construction-site words on paper. Stop when there are about twenty-five words on the list. Cut out the words to create strips, one word on each strip. Fold the strips of paper and put them in a container. Have each child draw a strip of paper from the container. Then challenge the children to write a short story or poem using the word they chose. When they are finished writing, invite the children to read their piece aloud.

Younger Children

Invite younger children to help you set up a "construction zone" outside in the sandbox area. Work with the children to determine what kinds of construction signs they might create to identify the construction zone. Invite children to experiment with re-creating the various phases of construction, from the foundation up. Involve children in selecting the materials they might use to show the different phases of construction. For example, they might collect stones and rocks for the foundation and clay or plaster to "cement" the rocks together. Ask the children what they might use to frame their buildings. Could they use sticks or blocks of wood? Add toy trucks and construction vehicles to the construction zone. Ask the children to determine who will do the various jobs at the site.

Create a construction-site word wall. Include new words the children have learned. Invite them to draw pictures that illustrate the words and place them on the word wall next to the corresponding words.

Each day, read a new book related to construction to the children. Afterward, review the book with them, looking for pictures or things they observed at the construction site. Do they remember the names of all of the things they saw?

Invite the children to make their own construction-site dictionaries. Make blank books by stapling sheets of paper together. Use colored construction paper for the front and back covers. Collect a variety of builders' supply catalogs. Have the children cut out pictures from the catalogs and glue them to the pages of their books. Work with the children to label the pictures in their books by writing the words for them to copy or writing on each page what they tell you about the picture.

On chart paper, create a class book about construction sites. Invite each child to contribute a sentence or two. Then write the story on separate sheets of paper, one or two sentences on each page. Have children choose pages to illustrate. Then staple the pages together. Ask the children what the title of the book should be. Write the title on the cover and add the book to the class library for the children to look at on their own.

Revisiting the Walk

All of the children will enjoy returning to the construction site periodically to check on its progress. Encourage older children to note the changes in their construction journals. Record what the younger children have to say about changes at the site. When you return from the walk, play back the recording to remind children what they said. Then have them draw pictures of the changes they observed.

Books

Adamson, Heather. 2004. *A day in the life of a construction worker.* Mankato, MN: Capstone Press.

Barton, Byron. 1990. *Building a house.* New York: HarperTrophy.

———. 1997. *Machines at work.* New York: HarperFestival.

Biard, Philippe. 1997. *Construction.* New York: Scholastic.

Gibbons, Gail. 1983. *New road!* New York: T.Y. Crowell.

———.1986. *Up goes the skyscraper!* New York: Four Winds Press.

———. 1990. *How a house is built.* New York: Holiday House.

Hennessy, B. G. 1997. *Road builders.* New York: Puffin.

Hoban, Tana. 1992. *Dig, drill, dump, fill.* New York: HarperCollins.

———. 1997. *Construction zone.* New York: HarperCollins.

Hudson, Cheryl Willes. 2006. *Construction zone.* Cambridge, MA: Candlewick Press.

Killey, Don. 2003. *At a construction site.* Toronto: Kids Can Press.

Pluckrose, Henry. 1998. *On a building site.* New York: Franklin Watts.

Radford, Derek. 1994. *Building machines and what they do.* Cambridge, MA: Candlewick Press.

Tarsky, Sue. 1997. *The busy building site.* New York: Putnam.

Neighborhood Walk

Before the Walk

The neighborhood around your center or school can be a fascinating place for children to explore, whether it consists of solely homes, homes and businesses, or a park, athletic field, and school. Before walking with the children, take some time to explore the learning opportunities your neighborhood can offer children. Make a list of the different buildings, outdoor environments, and things that might be of interest to the children. Think of questions to ask during the walk. Initiate discussions with the children beforehand about neighborhoods—what they are, how they are the same and different, and what the children's own neighborhoods are like. If children have their own questions about neighborhoods, be sure to write them down and bring the list with you during the walk. This is also an opportunity to discuss the variety of homes people live in and what "home" means to children. Besides people, do animals live in the neighborhood too? Where are the animals' homes? A very good book to spark discussion is *A House Is a House for Me* by Mary Ann Hoberman.

Walks around the neighborhood allow children to

- pay closer attention to the things they pass by every day

- see how neighborhoods are the same and different

- explore the concept of a "neighborhood community"

- observe the people in neighborhoods and the kinds of jobs they perform

- notice how a neighborhood might change if new buildings, businesses, or homes are built

- wonder how a neighborhood might change during certain times of the year

Words to Use and Learn

apartment	gas station	library	post office
athletic club	grocery store	mall	restaurant
clinic	home improvement store	office	school
community center		park	signs and billboards
drug store	hospital	parking lot	traffic signal/traffic
	house		

Things to Bring on the Walk

✔ a spiral notebook that includes the children's questions and notes about experiences that might interest them (provocations), and for noting your observations of the children during the walk

✔ a camera

✔ clipboards and paper for the children

✔ writing and drawing tools

✔ a tape recorder or other recording device

✔ backpacks or paper bags for collecting things

✔ measuring tools, such as tape measures, rulers, or string

During the Walk

Your walk will be guided by the things that are available to explore in your neighborhood as well as the children's interests. Each neighborhood is different, and the suggested activities below are just a sampling of the learning opportunities available during a walk through the neighborhood. Children pass through the neighborhood every day on their way to the center or school, but chances are they have not noticed all of the things it encompasses. During the walk, encourage them to look for things they may not have noticed before. Write down the things younger children observe; for older children, have them keep their own lists of their new observations.

Encourage the children to be aware of the sounds and smells in the neighborhood. Is the neighborhood relatively quiet or is it a busy area with sounds of cars, buses, and people? Are there construction noises? Is the neighborhood noisier or quieter during certain times of the day? Be sure to record the sounds of the neighborhood for children to listen to after the walk. What do the children smell in the neighborhood? Are there restaurants or fast-food outlets, and can the children smell food cooking? Is there a bakery? Does the amount of traffic affect the air quality? Do the vehicles and machines at construction sites emit specific smells? What do gas stations smell like?

Be aware of items that may be appropriate for children to collect, such as flyers or neighborhood newspapers as well as items from nature, such as leaves and pebbles. If there is an area where children can sit comfortably, consider having them sit and draw pictures of or write about what they see.

Observing and Speculating about Homes

Notice the number of and types of homes in the neighborhood. Are there single-family homes, apartment buildings, duplexes, or condos? What materials are the homes made of? What colors are they? How are the homes similar to or different from the children's own homes? Older children may want to keep track of how many people they think live in the neighborhood based on the number of residences they see.

Do the homes have garages attached? How many? Can you tell whether children live in the homes by the things in the yard, such as play structures or riding toys? Can you tell whether pets live in the homes? Are there fences around the yards? Do any contain doghouses? Are there cars parked in the street in front of the homes or apartments? Is there underground parking beneath the apartment buildings?

If your neighborhood consists primarily of homes, have children help keep track of specific details related to the homes. For example, younger children can count the number of homes and their colors; front doors and their colors; windows that are open and windows with blinds or curtains closed; yards with fences. How many homes have mailboxes out front?

Observing and Speculating about Businesses

What are the different types of businesses in the neighborhood? Have older children keep lists of the different businesses during the walk; keep a list of the different businesses younger children suggest. Do they know what goes on in the different businesses? Are there more retail stores that offer services, such as clinics or hair salons, or are there more businesses, such as law firms and corporate offices? Are there any businesses children haven't noticed before? For children unable to read businesses' signs, how can they tell what the businesses are? Are some signs bigger or easier to see than others?

Talk about the importance of location and the need for certain items or services offered by businesses. Do some businesses seem to have more customers than others? Why? Is it because of what the businesses sell or offer? Is it because of the location of the business, for example, on a busy street versus a side street? Are there two or more of the same type of business in the neighborhood? Does one business attract more customers than another? Do many businesses have their own parking lots? Are the lots large or small?

Observing and Speculating about Athletic Fields, Parks, and Other Open Spaces

Is the neighborhood filled with homes or businesses, or are there open spaces, such as parks and playing fields? Identify the different open spaces. Is there a school? Does it have an athletic field nearby? What type of field is it? Is it a soccer field, football field, or baseball field? Is anyone playing on the field or working on it? What kinds of things do people who maintain athletic fields do? Can the children tell by the outdoor area surrounding the school whether the school is an elementary school, middle school, or high school? How does the area surrounding an elementary school look different from the area surrounding a high school?

Is the open space a park? How big is the park? What does the park contain? Are there picnic tables, playing fields, paved areas, such as basketball courts, playground equipment, and public restrooms? Are there many trees? Is there a wooded area nearby? How many people are in the park? What are they doing? Are there areas for dogs to run and play (dog parks)? Are there any wild animals or birds?

Are there other open areas, such as fields or construction areas? What type of fields are they? Is food, such as corn or wheat, grown in the fields? Does the space appear to be abandoned or not used for anything in particular? Why is that? Is there construction going on in the open space? What is being torn down or built?

Are open or green spaces important in neighborhoods? Why or why not? Is there a community garden in the neighborhood? What is a community garden? Who takes care of it and who can have the flowers and vegetables grown in the garden?

After the Walk

Gather the children for a discussion of all the things they observed from the walk around the neighborhood. Ask what interested them the most. What did they notice that they hadn't seen before? Ask them to describe the neighborhood. Are there mostly homes or mostly businesses in the neighborhood? Is it a quiet or a busy neighborhood? Review any notes you may have written about the children's observations. Did the children keep a tally of the number of homes versus the number of businesses? What do the numbers tell them about the type of neighborhood it is?

Older Children

Spend some time with older children to get a sense of the things that most interested them about the neighborhood walk. What were some of the activities they seemed most involved in? Did they sketch anything or jot down notes? What could they construct that might demonstrate some of their observations or discoveries about the neighborhood? Do they have any concerns about the neighborhood, such as about a vacant lot or a busy intersection? Are there things they can do to research their concerns and follow up on them?

Invite the children to work together to create a map of the neighborhood using long sheets of paper. Encourage children to think about distances and scale. They may need to revisit the walk to write down street names and the names of businesses as well as the number of buildings on each block or street. Display the completed map at the children's eye level.

Invite children to consider the difference between a *house* and a *home*. Both words mean the same thing—or do they? How is a house different from a home? Does one word have more emotions attached to it than another? Encourage children to write about what the two words mean to them.

Is there such a thing as a "perfect neighborhood"? What would a perfect neighborhood look like? Have the children describe what a perfect neighborhood means to them.

People's perceptions of the same things or events can be very different. Have the children think of an event or something they all observed from the walk. Then invite them to write their impressions of it. Afterward, have the children read their pieces aloud. How were the children's descriptions or observations the same or different? What does that say about the way people perceive things?

Younger Children

After the walk, gather the children to talk about the events or sights that particularly interested them. Young children can quickly become captivated by the simplest things, and chances are they have many details to share. On a sheet of chart paper, list the things children share about the walk. After they have shared, read the list back to them, acknowledging all of their observations, and the length of their list. ("You created a very long list!") Save the list and revisit it when you need ideas for activities or ways children might document their learning from the neighborhood walk.

Add new words to an existing word wall.

Collect books on things that interested the children during the walk, such as grocery stores, restaurants, different types of homes, or green spaces. Read a different book to them each day.

Add items to the block area to create a miniature version of the neighborhood. Begin by asking the children to help you make a list of the different types of buildings they observed during the walk, such as schools, gas stations, apartment buildings, video stores, and hair salons. Tell the children that most buildings or businesses have names, and ask the children what names they might give the buildings listed. Write the names on index cards.

Collect shoe boxes or other small boxes to add to the block area to represent the neighborhood buildings. Have the children decorate the boxes and tape the corresponding labels to the boxes. Invite the children to re-create the neighborhood in the block area using the box buildings and anything else you may have collected, such as toy people and vehicles.

Make blank books by folding sheets of paper in half and stapling a construction-paper cover over them. Place the blank books in the writing center and invite the children to use writing and drawing tools to create books about what they saw during the walk through the neighborhood.

 **Revisiting the Walk**

Consider making a walk through the neighborhood part of your regular routine. Discuss with the children in advance things they might want to look for. But always be on the lookout for any unexpected learning opportunities that happen to capture the children's attention.

Books

Bailey, Debbie. 1998. *The playground.* Willowdale, ON: Annick Press.

Desimin, Lisa. 1997. *My house.* New York: Henry Holt.

Emberley, Rebecca. 1990. *My house: A book in two languages / Mi casa: un libro en dos lenguas.* Boston: Little, Brown.

Granowsky, Alvin. 2001. *At the park.* Brookfield, CT: Cooper Beech Press.

Hill, Mary. 2003. *Signs at the park.* New York: Scholastic.

Hoberman, Mary Ann. 1978. *A house is a house for me.* New York: Viking.

Holland, Gini. 2004. *I live in a town.* Milwaukee, WI: Weekly Reader Library.

Lee, Huy Voun. 1998. *In the park.* New York: Henry Holt.

Pancella, Peggy. 2005. *I live in a suburb.* Chicago: Heinemann Library.

——. 2006. *I live in a town.* Chicago: Heinemann Library.

Salzmann, Mary Elizabeth. 2005. *We are at the park.* Edina, MN: ABDO Publishing.

Treays, Rebecca. 1998. *My town.* Tulsa, OK: Educational Development Corp.

——. 1999. *My street.* Tulsa, OK: Educational Development Corp.

Trumbauer, Lisa, and Gail Saunders-Smith. 2005. *Living in a small town.* Mankato, MN: Capstone Press.

——. 2005. *Living in a suburb.* Mankato, MN: Capstone Press.

See also the City Plaza Walk book list for books about business you may have in your neighborhood.

Fire Station Walk

Before the Walk

Most visits to fire stations will be part of a scheduled tour, since fire departments everywhere offer extensive community outreach programs. Firefighters will often demonstrate their specialized equipment to children. Looking at this huge equipment up close is impressive and so is seeing how everything is carefully planned for quick action. Trips to the fire station give children an opportunity to

- **observe several types of emergency vehicles up close and perhaps look inside them**

- **learn about the work that firefighters do and see their uniforms and firefighting clothes**

- **examine the various parts of the equipment, such as hoses, hooks and belts, ladders, and oxygen tanks**

- **discover how the equipment is stored, taken care of, and kept ready for action**

- **look around inside the fire station and perhaps hear the emergency alarms, loudspeakers, sirens, walkie-talkies, and other equipment**

Walking to a specific destination, such as a fire station, will mean more to the children—especially younger children—if they have some information about that place beforehand. A fire station may not be a place to drop in on for follow-up visits and questions. It is a good idea to have all your questions in mind before your trip so you can get them answered by the firefighter who shows you around.

Depending on the children's knowledge of fire stations, read and discuss books about firefighters and fire stations. *Fire Stations* by Jason Cooper and *I'm Going to Be a Firefighter* by Edith Kunhardt are good general introductions. *Fire! Fire!* by Gail Gibbons has wonderful information about fighting fires in a variety of settings and shows the vehicles in action. Both this book and Gibbons's *Emergency!* label parts of the fire trucks and other vehicles to help you point these things out to the children. Look for other books that have good pictures of vehicles and have them on display.

Talk about how firefighters have special jobs to do and how they work as a team. Even after reading books about firefighters, you will have questions, so start assembling a list to ask at the fire station. Become familiar with the large variety of equipment in use today; this will help the children recognize some of it and assimilate what the firefighter shows and tells them. It will also help you to notice things to point out to the children, focus attention, and reinforce the things you discussed and saw in the books.

Words to Use and Learn

alarm	dispatcher	gloves	pole
ambulance	fire extinguisher	helmet	pumper engine
ax	firefighter	hose	searchlight
boots	fire hydrant	ladder truck	siren
chief	fire truck	oxygen tank and mask	tanker truck

Things to Bring on the Walk

✓ a spiral notebook that includes the children's questions and notes about experiences that might interest them (provocations), and for noting your observations of the children during the walk

✓ a camera

✓ clipboards and paper for the children

✓ writing and drawing tools

✓ backpacks or paper bags for collecting things

✓ tape recorder or other recording device

During the Walk

Look at the fire station building as you arrive and notice objects that tell you it is a fire station. Is there a name or number on the building and are there any vehicles outside? Are there large garage-type doors and are the driveways kept clear? Do you see writing on the vehicles that tell you what they are or whose they might be? Are there loudspeakers, lights, alarms, or sirens on top of the building? Can you tell how many floors there are in the building and whether it looks new or old? Guess whether or not it has a pole. Are there other doors besides the garage-type doors?

When you enter the building, notice how huge the fire engines look and all the equipment lined up around the room. Notice that the firefighters' working suits (coats and pants) are hanging, ready to use. Are there pants with boots inside them ready for a firefighter to jump into? This system of the pants placed over the boots is called a Quick Hitch—it might work well for preschoolers' snow pants and boots.

Notice belts, hooks, packs, helmets, gloves, oxygen tanks, and anything else that is ready to go. A tour leader will probably tell you about the things you are seeing and may demonstrate how quickly firefighters put on their work clothes. The leader may let your group feel the helmets, coats, boots, and gloves. The pieces of clothing are heavier than they look. The leader will also tell you about the equipment and point out the hoses, ladders, and parts of the fire trucks and other vehicles. Look at the dials and gauges on the trucks and have the firefighter explain what the dials or gauges tell or do. Look at the controls on the truck and any other special equipment.

Notice the lights on the engines. How many of the engines are like ones you looked at in the books? Do you see an ambulance or rescue unit, and are there stretchers, splints, and other emergency equipment on or near it? Notice extra ladders and hoses around the station. Do firefighters load those on the trucks? Are there extra sets to use when hoses are being cleaned? Ask how the hoses are cleaned and dried. Ask how they decide what kind of trucks they need. Wonder if all the trucks have their own water, how the hoses go up with the ladders, or whether the ladders have pipes on them. In addition, ask any questions from your list.

Notice other things inside the station. Are there living quarters in this station? Is there a kitchen or lounge area, lockers for storage, an office, and a pole? Do you see people working in an office or taking care of equipment? Are there pictures, posters, or information about fire prevention on display?

Do All Fire Station Have Poles?

Not all fire stations have poles, especially some of the newer ones where the living quarters are not above the station, or stations that do not have living quarters because they use volunteer or part-time firefighters. If you are visiting a station that looks like it is on one level, don't expect to see a pole. In stations that have poles, what safety procedure do they have to make sure no one falls down the hole?

Do they have a Dalmatian dog at the fire station? Some fire stations still have dogs as mascots as some books suggest, but not for the jobs that the Dalmatians used to do when horses pulled fire wagons.

Why are the colors of fire engines changing?

Counting at Fire Stations

There are many things to count all over the station, starting with the number of doors. Count the number of vehicles in the station. On one vehicle, count the number of tires, lights, ladders, hoses, bells, horns, dials, windows, and seats. Talk about why there are so many lights on the fire engines. Count the number of working outfits. Are all the outer garments hung near the engines or stored in other places as well? Ask how many people ride on each engine.

  Using the Senses

Talk about how shiny all the fire engines look. Touch them and feel the slick metal panels. Feel the bumpy parts on the steps and climbing areas; explain that the bumpy ridges on the steps will make them less slippery when climbing in and out.

If the firefighter turns on any of the alarms or lights, have the children cover their ears. Talk about how loud the alarms sound and how bright all the lights are. Talk about any scary feelings children might have being close to fire engines, but emphasize how firefighters work hard to keep people safe and save lives when there is a fire.

Keeping Safe

The firefighter may tell the children a little about keeping safe and preventing fires and may have special information on good rules for being safe. They may talk about Stop, Drop, and Roll if children's clothes catch fire. Collect all the fire safety materials they have available to use when you return from the walk. Some fire departments have a fire safety curriculum especially for young children, and if yours does, you may want to use it. Fire prevention education is an important part of making our communities safer. Firefighters know better than anyone how dangerous playing with matches and fire can be and welcome your help in getting that message out.

After the Walk

Children of all ages are likely to have much to talk about after the walk, especially if this is their first visit to a fire station. Ask each child what he or she liked best. What did the children learn that they didn't know before? What do they think it would be like to be a firefighter?

Older Children

Fire safety is an important part of any discussion involving fire stations and the work of firefighters. Older children may be interested in creating public safety messages of their own to post around the school or center, such as posters that show the importance of Stop, Drop, and Roll.

For children who are interested in creating artwork relating to a fire station, suggest that children pretend they are sculptors who have been commissioned to create a statue in front of a fire station. What kind of sculpture would they create?

Invite children to write books titled "A Day in the Life of a Firefighter."

Encourage children to write their own books about fire safety to take home and share with their families.

Examine fire hydrants in your area. See if the children can figure out where the fire hoses attach and where the controls might be. Wonder how the firefighters open the hydrants and make them work. How far apart are the fire hydrants? Are all fire hydrants the same? If not, what are the differences? Could firefighters use the water from several hydrants to fight a big fire?
Have interested children research the history of firefighting, including information about some of the earliest equipment used.

Firefighters work to put out fires, but are children aware how important fire was to the first humans? Have children research when the first humans discovered they could create fire. Then have children write their own versions of the discovery of fire.

Younger Children

Younger children may be interested in creating a large mural of a fire station. Collect a variety of objects for them to use for their mural, such as construction paper and paint. Also include three-dimensional items, such as string or narrow ribbon for hoses, and dark-colored plastic for coats, boots, and helmets.

Invite children to convert some of the trucks in the block area to fire trucks. Ask them what types of materials they might need for the conversion, such as handmade ladders and small pieces of plastic tubing. Work with the children to find the items, then allow children plenty of time to create their fire trucks.

Add new words learned from the walk to the fire station to an existing word wall.

Ask the children about some of the things they learned related to fire safety. Help children create posters or booklets about fire safety. For children who are not yet writing, write exactly what they tell you about fire safety onto their posters or in their booklets. Ask all children to illustrate their posters or booklets using crayons or paints.

Reread any books about fire stations you read earlier to see whether all of the children's questions have been answered. Talk about other types of firefighting vehicles besides trucks, such as fire boats, helicopters, planes, and trucks for airport fires.

Take a "Fire Walk" around the room. First, have children identify all of the things in the room that begin with the letter F (add any new words that begin with F to the word wall). Next, have children identify all of the things in the room that are hot or could potentially be hot. Be sure to reinforce safety by reminding children of the hot items they should not touch at any time.

 ## Revisiting the Walk

Have a Fire Safety Day at your center or school. Consider inviting some of the firefighters from the fire station you visited to come to see all of the things the children did and made to help prepare for the event.

Also, look around inside for fire extinguishers, smoke detectors, alarm systems, and anything else that seems to be connected to fire safety or prevention. Think of questions to ask the firefighters about these items. Do they use anything like the fire extinguishers that are found in homes or schools? Wonder when those types of chemical or foam materials should be used, and when you should just use water. Do the firefighters ever get false alarms from building alarm systems that go off when there is not a real fire? What can make alarm systems go off by mistake?

Books

Abramson, Andra Serlin. 2007. *Fire engines up close.* New York: Sterling.

Bingham, Caroline. 1995. *Fire truck.* Mighty machines. London: Dorling Kindersley.

Butler, Dori Hillestad, and Joan C. Waites. 2007. *F is for firefighting.* Gretna, LA: Pelican.

Cooper, Jason. 1992. *Fire stations.* Vero Beach, FL: Rourke Corp.

Dubois, Muriel L., and Anne McMullen. 2003. *Out and about at the fire station.* Minneapolis, MN: Picture Window Books.

Gibbons, Gail. 1984. *Fire! Fire!* New York: Crowell.

———.1994. *Emergency!* New York: Holiday House.

Hoena, B. A. 2004. *The fire station.* Pebble plus. Mankato, MN: Capstone Press.

Kalman, Bobbie. 2004. *Firefighters to the rescue!* New York: Crabtree Pub. Co.

Kunhardt, Edith. 1989. *I'm going to be a fire fighter.* Read with me paperbacks. New York: Scholastic.

Moignot, Daniel. 1999. *Fire fighting.* A first discovery book. New York: Scholastic.

Rickert, Janet Elizabeth, and Pete McGahan. 2000. *Russ and the firehouse.* Special needs collection. Bethesda, MD: Woodbine House.

Rockwell, Anne F. 2003. *At the firehouse.* New York: HarperCollins.

Saunders-Smith, Gail. 1998. *The fire station.* Mankato, MN: Pebble Books.

Zimmerman, Andrea Griffing, David Clemesha, and Karen Barbour. 2003. *Fire! fire!, hurry! hurry!* New York: Greenwillow Books.

Farm Walk

Before the Walk

Before your farm walk, find out from the children what they already know about farms. Have they been to a farm before? Do any friends or relatives have farms? If so, what do they have on their farm or what do they grow? For younger children who have never been to a farm, read several books to them before the walk to give them a knowledge base and vocabulary they might not know, such as the names of farm animals, machinery, and crops. *Farm* by Angela Leeper is a wonderful book to start with. For all children, ask what questions they have about farms. Be sure to jot the questions down in a notebook to revisit during the walk or afterward.

A trip to a farm offers children opportunities to

- **observe the animals that live on farms, what size they are, and where they live during the day and at night**

- **discover how animals are fed, what they eat, and where their food is kept**

- **wonder about the food farmers grow for their animals and for people**

- **watch farmers completing chores, such as milking cows or goats and collecting eggs**

- **see various crops growing and being harvested**

- **study the machines farmers use, their sizes, and perhaps how they work**

- **notice the land and buildings on the farm and what they are used for**

Words to Use and Learn

bales	dairy farm	hay/hayloft	seeds
barn	farmers market	herd	silo
combine	fence	pasture	soil
compost	grain	pitchfork	tractor
crops	harvest	plow	

the names of any farm animals you will see

Things to Bring on the Walk

✔ a spiral notebook that includes the children's questions and notes about experiences that might interest them (provocations), and for noting your observations of the children during the walk

✔ a camera

✔ clipboards and paper for the children

✔ writing and drawing tools

✔ backpacks or paper bags for collecting things

✔ a tape recorder or other recording device

✔ measuring tools, such as tape measures, rulers, or string

During the Walk

Consider using some of the following suggestions during the walk to help children learn about farms. Should children discover other aspects of the farm that interest them, be sure to help them pursue and later document those interests.

Observing at Farms

Notice that some really large areas of land have fences around them for the animals, and that some large tracts are planted fields or plowed fields waiting to be planted. Do you see any silos or barns in the distance? Point them out to the children and talk about their shape and color and what they are used for. Since these buildings are usually quite large, they are easier to see in their entirety from a distance. Do you see some smaller buildings as well? Plan to find out what is in all the buildings you see. Can you tell where the people on the farm live?

Notice the mailboxes along the road and how far apart they are and how far from the houses they may be. Think about how the people get their mail each day.

Notice how all the buildings are laid out at the farm. Are there fenced-in areas next to buildings that house animals so the animals can go outside? Are there any animals roaming around outdoors? Do you see animals eating or people feeding them? Where is the animals' food stored or prepared? Are there separate buildings for different animals?

Look in the barn to see what is there. Are there stalls for animals? Are there open spaces and a

hayloft? Notice special features and everything else in the barn—from a rope swing to bales of hay, pitchforks or other implements, or feeding areas. In all the buildings, observe the arrangements and procedures for feeding the animals and notice how they are adapted to the animal's size and way of eating. Do you see egg collection areas by the chickens? Are there milking machines for cows or goats? Can someone show you how cows are milked? Is there a special place for milking?

Observe as many food products growing as you can. Notice vegetable patches and corn or grain fields; try to take the children close to these areas so they can see how high the corn is and whether the plants have ears. Point out how vegetables grow either on plants, vines, or in the ground. What else do you see growing (flowers, grains)? Show the children as many different types of grain as you can. Talk about where they have heard their names. The wheat and oats they see will not look much like the cereals they eat so you will have to explain the connection later.

Watch farmers using equipment and talk about the jobs the machines do on the farm. Notice how large and complicated many of the machines are. Does the farmer have his or her own equipment or is some equipment shared with other farmers? Where is the equipment stored? Do you see fuel tanks for use on the farm? (Farmers usually cannot take their machines to a gas station.) Are there gas pumps or hoses attached to the tanks? Point out where the gas goes into the tractor and think about how it gets there. How much gas can the tractor hold and how often does the farmer have to fill it? How long can it run on a tank of gas? Notice how some machines attach to tractors to do their jobs. Do you see different-size tractors? Does the size of the tractor have anything to do with how much gas it can hold and how much gas it uses?

Be sure to take plenty of photographs of the farm and of the children doing various things on the farm, such as petting the animals or standing near the farmer and some of the farm equipment.

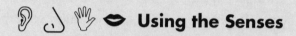 **Using the Senses**

Listen to the sounds on the farm. Do the animals make sounds like the ones we always say they make? What animal sounds do the children hear? Record some of the sounds to play when you return. What other sounds do they hear besides animal sounds? Ask the children to identify as many as they can.

What smells do the children notice on the farm? Are there different smells in the different animal areas? Can the children smell the hay either in bales, in the barn, or as it is being cut? Is there a smell of the animals' food as it is served or being made? Which animals seem to be the smelliest? Are there different smells indoors and outdoors in the animal areas?

Are there any animals the children can touch? What do their coats feel like? Do the baby animals feel different from the adult ones? What does hay feel like?

Does the farmer have any food items children can sample? Food items will be seasonal, such as peas and berries in the summer and apples in the fall. Talk with the children about when certain foods are in season. Tell the children that even though they may see a particular food item in the grocery store that doesn't mean it's in season. If a store has berries during the fall or winter, for example, it means those foods were produced somewhere else in the world—in warmer climates or in climates that produce the food year-round.

Identifying Things at Farms

Tell the children the names of as many different kinds of farm implements, machines, and animals as you know. Explain that animals are called different names when they are young than when they are grown up (just like boys and girls become men and women) and have different names if they are male or female. Ask the farmer to help you with the identification if you are not sure what things are called.

Identify the separate buildings and parts of buildings, such as a chicken house or coop, granary, silo, and hayloft. Again ask the farmer to tell you the correct names for parts of the farm. Do the feeding areas have names? Do the working areas, such as the milking stations, have special names? What about places where eggs are collected or hatched?

Don't be embarrassed to ask what things are called. Farming has become highly technical and mechanized and people not involved in farming have no idea what many things are. Point out the few familiar implements, such as a pitchfork, which may be similar to things children have seen before.

Counting and Measuring

Ask children to count all the buildings they see and the number of doors into some of the buildings. Ask why there are so many doors. Count the stalls for different animals and the number of areas for baby animals. Count the number of fenced-in areas.

Count how many people children see working and the number of different machines they see. Are there large and small versions of some of the machines? Count wheels or other machine parts.

Can children count the animals, or is it too hard because they keep moving? Maybe they can count baby animals. Take photos of clusters of animals to count and identify later.

Measure how high the plants are. Measure how high things come up on you and on the children. Do the children have to reach over their heads to measure some things? What plants grow the tallest? Write down some of the size comparisons of the different plants as well as other findings.

Count how many ears of corn are on a corn stalk, or pumpkins on a vine. Let the children think of other things they would like to count or measure.

Wondering about Farms

Wonder what it must feel like to be up in the hayloft. If some children live on the farm, they may be able to tell you. Wonder how the hay gets up there and how people get up there.

Wonder what it feels like to ride on a tractor—especially a very big one. Wonder if the farmer gets tired of having to take care of the animals every single day, since there are no weekends or time off from feeding or milking animals. Does the farmer ever take a vacation? What happens to the animals if he or she leaves for a while?

Wonder whether the animals ever get lost and how the farmer finds them. Wonder how they keep the animals from climbing over fences and getting out. Are there different kinds of fences for different animals?

Wonder what can make problems for the farmer. What does he or she do in really bad weather? What things can harm the crops?

Collecting Items

Bring back a collection of dried grains, corn, straw, corn shafts, and any other dried weeds or plants to use in collages.

A Safety Note
Before approaching a field, ask the farmer if it has recently been sprayed with insecticide, herbicide, or fertilizer. If it has been, be careful not to expose the children to the area.

After the Walk

Children who have never visited a farm before are apt to be very excited to share their experiences. Notice what seemed to fascinate them the most and make a note of it. Also discuss the things they didn't like so much and what things would be hard for them if they lived on a farm. Do they think they would like living on a farm? Your notes may be helpful later when children are deciding ways to document their learning.

Don't forget to write a group thank-you note to the farmer or family who showed you around the farm. Include individual children's comments and have them draw pictures of things they saw on the farm.

Older Children

Older children may enjoy making farm-animal puppets from small paper bags or farm-animal masks from paper plates. Put out a collection of small paper plates; construction paper; scrap pieces of wallpaper in browns, pinks, and other animal colors and textures; small pieces of yarn; curls of crepe paper; cotton balls; crayons and markers; and glue. The children can use their puppets or masks to make up and present farm stories or to give information about the animals to the younger children.

Invite the children to think about all of the tasks performed on farms and whether farmers have all the equipment they need to perform the tasks. What new farm equipment do children think would help them? Invite children to write about

and draw pictures of the new farm equipment, giving each piece a name and explaining how it would help farmers.

Have children choose a crop they saw on the farm. Then ask them to write about the steps involved in bringing it from the farm to our table. Some children will need to do research to ensure they aren't omitting key steps in the process. Also have them estimate how long the entire process takes. For example, how many days does it take for a tomato to go from the farm to our table?

Invite children to make up riddles involving things they observed on the farm, including farm equipment, farm animals, and crops. After they've written their riddles, have them read them to the class to see if other children know the answers.

The activities that happen on farms are mostly determined by the seasons. Have children think about how the activities and daily chores on a farm change from season to season. Then have children make a list of activities by season—fall, winter, spring, and summer. Are there other jobs that are affected by the seasons? What are they? How are they affected? Have children make a list of other jobs that are affected by the seasons.

Younger Children

What kinds of things did the younger children collect at the farm? Can any of the items be glued on paper to make collages? Grains, corn kernels, and other plant parts make great collage items.

Children can also draw pictures of crops and plants on their collages or tear out pictures of them from magazines to glue to their collages.

Invite children to make a farm mural from large sheets of paper. Besides painting and drawing on the mural, they can also glue collected items, such as hay and grains, to the paper. Gather furry fabric scraps for children to use for the farm animals' coats and denim and flannel for the farmer's clothes.

Listen to the recording you made during the walk. Have children identify the sounds of the animals or other sounds they heard.

Write new words on an existing word wall or create a new word wall of farm words.

Have the children help create farm buildings to add to the block area. Buildings can be made from a variety of medium-size boxes and containers, such as shoe boxes, round oatmeal containers, and half-pint milk cartons. Ask the children to identify some of the farm buildings they saw and which boxes or containers could be used to create them. After the buildings are constructed, children can paint them. When the buildings are dry, add them to the block area along with toy farm animals and vehicles.

Play guessing games using vegetables, grains, animals, and machines seen on the farm. Give a short description of the item and see whether the children can guess it. If not, add more information until they do. If possible, try to have replicas on hand (for example, toy tractors and farm animals and real produce items) to show children after they have guessed the items.

 **Revisiting the Walk**

If possible, try to revisit the farm each season to note changes and how the seasons affect life on the farm. Encourage older children to begin keeping "farm journals" to document the changes they see. Help younger children by writing down the changes they observed after you've returned from the walk. Then they can draw pictures of the things next to their words.

 **Books**

Bingham, Carol. 2004. *Tractor.* New York: Dorling Kindersley.

Bridges, Sarah, and Amy Bailey Muehlenhardt. 2006. *I drive a tractor.* Minneapolis: Picture Window Books.

Brown, Margaret Wise, and Felicia Bond. 1989. *Big red barn.* New York: Harper & Row.

Cabrera, Jane. 2008. *Old MacDonald had a farm.* New York: Holiday House.

Duvoisin, Roger. 1963. *Veronica goes to Petunia's farm.* London: Bodley Head.

Elliott, David, and Holly Meade. 2008. *On the farm.* Cambridge, MA: Candlewick Press.

Fleming, Denise. 1994. *Barnyard banter.* New York: Henry Holt.

Fowler, Allan. 2000. *Living on farms.* Rookie read-about geography. New York: Children's Press.

Gibbons, Gail. 2007. *The vegetables we eat.* New York: Holiday House.

Kerr, Janet. 2000. *The quiet little farm.* New York: Henry Holt.

Leeper, Angela. 2004. *Farm.* Heinemann read and learn. Chicago: Heinemann Library.

Mitton, Tony, and Ant Parker. 2003. *Tremendous tractors.* Amazing machines. Boston: Kingfisher/Houghton Mifflin Co.

Pluckrose, Henry Arthur, and Teri Gower. 1998. *On the farm.* New York: F. Watts.

Saunders-Smith, Gail. 1999. *The farm.* Mankato, MN: Pebble Books.

Sweeney, Alyse. 2007. *Let's visit a dairy farm.* Scholastic news nonfiction readers. New York: Children's Press.

Apple Orchard Walk

Before the Walk

Most orchards are well organized for visitors and can accommodate various size and age groupings, making them an ideal site to visit. Because of the popularity of this trip, reservations are a must and should be made early. When you call, check on facilities for snacks and what they provide or have available. (Make a timetable or schedule for your visit so you can prepare for possible delays.) Find out whether the children will be walking or riding in carts so you can let the children know what to expect.

There are many different types of orchards. Large working operations may have a lot of machinery to aid in their work, and they may also do much of their own processing and baking. Smaller operations provide opportunities to pick your own apples. Some orchards have other products available as well, such as pumpkins, other fruits, and apple products, while others have hayrides or other attractions.

Many of the procedures and activities suggested for this trip can be easily adapted to visiting other similar places, such as a pumpkin patch, strawberry patch, orange grove, or other fruit orchard. Adapt the vocabulary words to suit the location.

Of course, the best time of year to visit an apple orchard is in the fall. Before your trip, however, you can do several activities with the children to heighten their awareness of apples and where they come from. You can also use discussions to identify questions the children may have about apple orchards. Be sure to write down their questions and bring them with you to the orchard.

Showing and Tasting Apples

For young children, bring in several kinds of apples in different colors and shapes (for example, Granny Smith, Golden Delicious, Red Delicious, and Macintosh). Talk about their color and shape and ask the children if they are all apples. After noticing their characteristics on the outside, cut the apples open and notice their core, flesh, and seeds. Do they look alike on the inside and do their seeds look alike? Cut the apples into small pieces and let the children feel their texture and taste them. Discuss the ways in which they are alike and different. Write down the children's observations about the apples and which ones they liked best. Explain that all apples grow on trees and that the type of apple depends on the type of tree. Plan to visit an orchard to see what types of trees and apples the orchard has and how their apples taste. Speculate about how apple growers can be sure they get the kind of apples they want. Do the apples ever get mixed up?

Talking about Apples

Ask the younger children what other things they like that might be made from apples. Bring in some apple juice and applesauce and discuss how these things might be made. Write down some questions the children have about things made from apples. For example, older children might ask, Where do they keep all the apples until they sell them or use them? How long will apples stay fresh, and how do they take care of them during that time? Where does the orchard send its apples? What problems can happen to hurt the apples (for example, frost, too much rain or not enough rain, and insects or worms), and how do they try to protect them? Why are some apples more expensive than others?

At the orchard, you and your group can

- see where apples come from and how they are picked and packaged

- learn about how an orchard works and how trees are cared for

- observe how apples are sorted, graded, and stored or processed for other uses

- taste different kinds of apples and learn something about the trees they grow on

- wonder about other products that are made from apples and see how some are made

- bring some apples back to eat or use

Words to Use and Learn

apple	cider	peck	skin
apple crate	core	peel	stem
apple picker	harvest	press	sweet
basket	juice	ripe	tart
bushel	ladder	seeds	tree

Things to Bring on the Walk

✓ a spiral notebook that includes the children's questions and notes about experiences that might interest them (provocations), and for noting your observations of the children during the walk

✓ a camera

✓ clipboards and paper for the children

✓ writing and drawing tools

✓ backpacks and paper bags for collecting things

✓ large canvas bags or plastic buckets to help carry the children's apples (paper bags often break)

✓ a tape recorder or other recording device

✓ measuring tools, such as tape measures, rulers, or string

 # During the Walk

Consider using some of the following suggestions during the walk to help children learn about apple orchards. Should children discover other aspects of the orchard that interest them, be sure to help them pursue and later document those interests.

Observing at Apple Orchards

Notice how the trees are planted. Are they in rows? Are there differences in the trees' heights, shapes, fullnesses, branch structures, and colors and textures of bark and leaves? Look carefully at the leaves to see how they grow. What happens to the branches when they are full of ripe apples? How are the trees organized? Are all the same kind of tree in one section? How many different kinds of trees does the orchard have? Watch how the apples are picked. Notice how careful the people are not to bruise or damage the apples. What special equipment is used to pick the apples?

How are the apples collected as they are being picked? How do they get from the trees to the buildings where they are sold or processed? Can you observe people or machines carrying apple crates to various places? Are there apples lying on the ground? Discuss how they got there and ask about what happens to them.

What buildings are there at the orchard? Is there a bakery where you can watch bakers making pies or other apple products? Is there a kitchen where you might see people making jelly, apple butter, or apple syrup? What machines do you see? What jobs do you see people doing?

Take photographs of the steps in the harvesting and sorting processes as you observe them to use in your follow-up activities.

Categorizing and Measuring

Watch how the apples are sorted. How do the workers decide what group each apple belongs in? What are the grades of apples and what do they mean? Besides type of apple, are they sorted by size, shape, weight, color, marks on them, or any other characteristics? Which parts of the sorting process are done by machines and which by people? How are the different categories of apples priced? Do you see other evidence of sorting on the shelves and in other parts of the showroom? Are there different-size baskets around? What does *peck* mean? How about *bushel*? Are there quarts, gallons, or pints for some of the apple products?

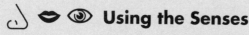 **Using the Senses**

How do the orchard and the buildings smell? Do the areas around the trees have any special smells? Are there good or bad smells and where do you think they come from? Can you smell things baking nearby, or are there other aromas in the processing and washing areas? Do the baskets of apples on display have a smell, and are there any differences among them?

Are there varieties of apples to taste? If possible, let the children taste several different kinds of apples. What differences do you notice? Talk about

how the apples taste; use words such as tart, sweet, and not so sweet. Are there differences in how firm or soft the apples are and does that affect the taste? Are there other things you can taste such as apple cider, apple butter, or apple jelly? Talk about how those things taste, and ask what is added to them that affects the taste.

Does the orchard feel like a happy place? How can you decide? How do the people who work there look? Do the children think it would be fun to work there?

Purchasing Items
Bring back different types of apples—some sweet, some tart, and in different colors (red, green, yellow). Besides simply enjoying the apples, some children may want to use the apples as models for art projects, such as drawings or paintings. Think about other items sold at the orchard that you might like to buy and taste later on, such as apple cider, apple jelly, apple butter, or apple syrup.

After the Walk

Talk about the trip, and let the children tell you all the things they remember and what parts were most interesting to them. If they could work at the orchard, what job would they like best? Do they still have unanswered questions about apples? If so, find out the answers to share with the children or have older children help discover the answers.

Older Children
View the photographs you took during the walk with the older children in the group. Ask what is happening in each photo. Were any events or experiences of particular interest to them? Ask the children open-ended questions to help them articulate what about the event or experience was so interesting.

Some children may have been surprised by all of the different kinds of apples. If you brought back a variety of apples, show them to the children again. Even though apples are similar in appearance, they have subtle differences. Have children describe what those differences are, such as color variations and different skin textures. Children could then make a detailed poster of all the different apples and label them with their names. Beneath the names of the apples they might list which apples are best suited for which kinds of foods, such as pies, applesauce, and cider.

Invite the children to write stories about apples from blossom to purchase at the orchard or store. If they know, they can include how long the various steps take.

Have the children ever heard the expression "An apple a day keeps the doctor away"? What does it mean? Are there other expressions children can think of that involve foods? Encourage children to begin keeping a list of food-related expressions and what they mean. They can have fun creating their own too.

Do the children know the story of Johnny Appleseed? Invite them to learn more about this real man whose mission it was to spread apples throughout the country.

Encourage the children to bring in their favorite apple recipes from home. Compile the recipes into an apple cookbook. Consider making some of the simpler recipes with the children. You can download apple recipes from the Redleaf Web site, www.redleafpress.org. Enter "Hey Kids!" into the search field and follow the links.

Younger Children

Show younger children the photographs you took. Ask them to tell you what is happening in each photo. Make extra copies so that the younger children can help you compile the photos to make a book of your walk to the apple orchard.

Invite each child to draw a picture of his or her favorite apple and label the drawings with the names of apples.

For a longer project, have children make apples from papier-mâché and when they are dry, paint them in their favorite colors. The apples could be added to fall harvest displays throughout the room.

Read books about apples and Johnny Appleseed to the children. Ask children open-ended questions about the story as you read to encourage them to think more about the story.

Add new vocabulary from the orchard visit to an existing word wall.

Invite the children to help you list all of the products made from apples that were sold at the orchard. Can they think of other apple products? Find magazine pictures of these products and make a large chart that shows apples and their products.

Sing songs, read poems, and perform fingerplays about apples with the children.

 **Revisiting the Walk**

Although fall is the best season to visit an apple orchard, consider visiting it in the spring and other times of the year as well. For example, in the spring, observe the beautiful blossoms on the trees and wonder how long it will be before the apples will appear. Encourage children to note their observations of the orchard at different times of the year in "apple journals."

Books

Bourgeois, Paulette, and Linda Hendry. 1990. *The amazing apple book.* Reading, MA: Addison-Wesley.

Flanagan, Alice K., and Romie Flanagan. 1999. *The Zieglers and their apple orchard.* New York: Children's Press.

Gibbons, Gail. 2000. *Apples.* New York: Holiday House.

Hall, Zoe. 1996. *The apple pie tree.* New York: The Blue Sky Press.

Landau, Elaine. 1999. *Apples.* A true book. New York: Children's Press.

Maestro, Betsy, and Giulio Maestro. 1992. *How do apples grow?* New York: HarperCollins.

Marzollo, Jean, and Judith Moffatt. 1997. *I am an apple.* New York: Scholastic.

Mayr, Diane, and Anne McMullen. 2003. *Out and about at the apple orchard.* Minneapolis: Picture Window Books.

Miller, Jane. 2000. *Farm alphabet book.* New York: Scholastic.

Patent, Dorothy Hinshaw, and William Munoz. 1990. *An apple a day: From orchard to you.* New York: Cobblehill Books/Dutton.

Rockwell, Anne F., and Lizzy Rockwell. 1989. *Apples and pumpkins.* New York: Macmillan.

Saunders-Smith, Gail. 1998. *Eating Apples.* Mankato, MN. Pebble Books.

Schaefer, Lola M. 2003. *Johnny Appleseed.* First biographies. Mankato, MN: Pebble Books.

Slawson, Michele Benoit, and Deborah Kogan Ray. 1994. *Apple picking time.* New York: Crown.

Wellington, Monica. 2001. *Apple Farmer Annie.* New York: Dutton Children's Books.

Concept Walks

"A tree with rocks and grass on a warm summer day"
Alexandra, age 4

What's It Made Of? Walk

Before the Walk

During this walk, you will be talking with the children about what the things around them are made of, such as buildings, roads, cars, signs, sidewalks, and statues. With older children, you may also talk about the distinction between natural materials and materials created by people. Therefore, have a few discussions with the children prior to the walk to help you determine their general knowledge base and vocabulary related to the materials used to create various things. Find out what they know about basic building materials, such as stone, brick, concrete, wood, metal, plastic, and glass. Discuss that these materials are used to create buildings and structures as well as pieces of art, such as statues and stained-glass windows. Do children know the difference between natural materials and manufactured materials? Have several examples on hand to show them, for example, wood, marble, metal, glass, and plastic. Examine different objects in the room and discuss what they are made of.

Depending on the location of your program, there may be a large variety of materials to discuss. If this is the case, you might preview the walk beforehand and decide to focus on only two or three materials at first. You can look for other materials during subsequent walks.

Walks that focus on what things are made of offer children opportunities to

- study different materials used to build or construct things and to create pieces of art

- discover why certain materials are chosen for certain purposes

- learn about natural materials and materials made by people

- develop a greater understanding of construction and construction processes

Natural and Manufactured Materials

Natural materials describe those materials produced in nature and that can be used with no alteration to their basic makeup. Some examples of natural materials are wood, marble, granite, limestone, gold, silver, platinum, and some types of glass.

Manufactured materials describe various "lab-grown" materials, or materials created by people. Many of these materials begin from natural materials that are processed, purified, and refined. For example, most metals begin in the form of ore, a natural material. After the ore is mined, the desired metal is extracted from the ore and processed, resulting in a new metal. Some examples of manufactured materials are brick, concrete, tile, steel, brass, bronze, aluminum, all plastics, and most glass.

Words to Use and Learn

aluminum	cinder block	hardwood	plastic
brass	concrete	iron	steel
brick	copper	limestone	stone
bronze	glass	marble	tile
carpentry	granite	metal	wood

Things to Bring on the Walk

✓ a spiral notebook that includes the children's questions and notes about experiences that might interest them (provocations), and for noting your observations of the children during the walk

✓ a camera

✓ clipboards and paper for the children

✓ writing and drawing tools

✓ backpacks or paper bags for collecting things

✓ measuring tools, such as tape measures, rulers, or string

✓ a tape recorder or other recording device

✓ small examples of various types of materials for the children's reference, such as tile pieces, granite or marble pieces, and wood scraps

During the Walk

Consider using some of the following suggestions during the walk to help children learn about different materials. Depending on the ages of the children in your group, you may need to individualize the learning opportunities to ensure they are appropriate for the children's level of development.

Be sure to take photographs or invite the children to draw pictures of how the different materials are used in different constructions or objects.

Examining Materials

Have younger children look for only one or two types of materials, such as stone and wood. Where do they see stone? Where do they see wood? Count how many times they see examples of wood and stone. Count how many times the materials appear on specific types of buildings, such as on homes, stores, or offices.

Do the children see stone and wood in their natural states, such as pebbles on the ground or the trunk of a tree? Stop and look at the examples you see and ask the children questions about the materials. What colors are the materials? Is all wood the same color? Is all stone the same color? If you see examples of marble or granite, ask children about the different colors that run through them. How many colors does the material contain?

What do the materials feel like? Are they cool, warm, smooth, or rough? Does the stone on a building feel different from stones on the ground? How does the wood of a door frame feel different from the wood (bark) of a tree?

Are there any construction sites nearby with stacked lumber or stone slabs? Can the children tell by the materials at the site what type of building is going up?

Do the children see the materials being used in something other than buildings or structures, such as statues, traffic signs or lights, or benches? Help the children keep a list of other ways the materials are used.

Older children might enjoy pairing up to look for examples of specific materials, such as stone, metal, wood, plastic, and glass. Give each pair a clipboard and pencils for keeping track of the number of times they see each of the materials. Also have children note how the material was used, such as a metal railing along steps or a large, wooden door into an apartment building. Do they see any materials they can't identify?

For each material, how many variations in color, texture, and temperature do they see or feel? How many different ways were the materials used, for example, was stone used as a walkway and also as a plaque on the side of an office building? Are there variations in texture and temperature among the different materials? Does the weather affect the temperature of any of the materials?

Wondering about Materials
How heavy are the materials? Are some heavier than others? Which ones? What types of machinery might be needed to move heavy materials into place? How do the materials stay in place?

Which materials are best suited for use outdoors? Which materials hold up in the rain, hot sun, or cold weather, including ice and snow? Which materials last the longest?

Which materials are best suited for which purposes? Which materials can best withstand very hot and very cold temperatures? Do the children see examples of materials that are breaking down or in need of repair? What are they? Why might they be breaking down?

Which materials might be easiest to work with? Why? Which materials might be the most and the least expensive? Why?

Which materials are environmentally friendly? Which materials are potentially harmful to the environment?

After the Walk

Discuss the children's findings by asking them how many different examples of materials they saw and how the materials were used. Ask the children which materials are better suited for which kinds of structures or objects and why. Were there more examples of natural materials or manufactured materials? What generalizations about each of the materials can the children make based on their findings? Be sure to share the photographs taken during the walk or have the children share any pictures they may have drawn.

Depending on the space available in your room, consider setting up stations or workshop areas where children can explore and work with the different materials, such as wood, metal, stone, and plastic. Besides an ample supply of the materials, you will also need to consider the types of tools needed to work with the materials. Art supplies, such as paint, crayons, paper, scissors, and glue, can also be added to the various stations. Encourage the children to combine materials in any way they desire. There will be no limit to where the children's creativity will take them—some may choose to create sculptures or other objects of art, while some may choose to create more functional objects, such as vehicles or balance scales. Be prepared to enhance and extend children's learning by adding new materials for them to work with or allowing them to work on their projects over the course of several days or weeks.

Older Children

Provide older children with resources to investigate where different materials come from or how they are made. Invite children to create books about specific materials, including information about the materials as well as magazine pictures or drawings. For example, a book about stone might be titled "All about Stone" and a book about plastic might be titled "All about Plastic." Children might also want to include the pros and cons of using certain materials such as the materials' effects on the environment.

Invite interested children to research the history of construction (stone-age construction, ancient construction, medieval construction, and modern-age construction) including the materials used by the earliest humans.

Check your local library or bookseller for the book *The Art of Construction* by Mario Salvadori. The book includes many hands-on activities that demonstrate the most basic construction principles such as tension and compression.

If you have set up workshop areas in the room that contain various types of materials, have the children help create word walls to post in each area. For example, the word wall in the metal workshop might contain a list of metals (copper, brass, gold, silver), metal-working terms (solder, hammer, melt, cool), and how metals are used (fixtures, hinges, keys, appliances).

Younger Children

Assist younger children as needed to enable them to learn about the different materials they saw on the walk. One idea would be to create bulletin boards dedicated to different materials. Invite children to find pictures of the materials in magazines or draw pictures to add to the bulletin boards. Include photographs from the walk.

Create a new word wall dedicated to materials used for construction and other creative works. Give it a title such as "What's It Made Of?" Have the children tell you when they've learned new words to add to the wall.

Create class books about construction and construction materials or materials used to create artwork. Review the materials the children saw during the walk. Invite them each to create a page for the book, focusing on one or two materials. Help the children write the names of the materials on the pages, if needed. Invite them to draw pictures of things made from those materials.

Add different, child-safe materials to the block area, such as plastic pipes, tiles pieces, and wood scraps. Put the new items in containers or bins and label them by type of material.

 ## Revisiting the Walk

Each time you go on a walk to look for different materials, chances are you and the children will discover examples you didn't notice on previous walks. Consider creating a chart with the names of the different materials written across the top.

Begin keeping track of how many times you see each material and where you saw it. Add to the chart after each walk. Ask the children whether everyone simply overlooked the material during previous walks or whether it's part of a new construction.

 **Books**

Braithwaite, Jill. 2004. *From tree to table.* Minneapolis: Lerner Publishing Group.

Davis, Gary W. 1997. *From rock to fireworks.* New York: Children's Press.

Knight, Bertram T. 1997. *From mud to house.* New York: Children's Press.

Kras, Sara Louise. 2004. *Metal.* Mankato, MN: Capstone Press.

———. 2004. *Wood.* Mankato, MN: Capstone Press.

Llewellyn, Claire. 2002. *Plastic.* New York: Franklin Watts.

Lucas, Rhonda Donald. 2002. *Plastic.* Mankato, MN: Capstone Press.

Marshal, Pam. 2003. *From tree to paper.* Minneapolis: Lerner Publishing Group.

Oxlade, Chris. 2001. *Plastic.* Chicago: Heinemann Library.

Ridley, Sarah. 2007. *A glass jar.* Milwaukee, WI: Gareth Stevens Publishing.

———. 2007. *A metal can.* How it's made. Milwaukee, WI: Gareth Stevens Publishing.

Royston, Angela. 2005. *How are things made?* Chicago: Heinemann.

Salvadori, Mario. 1990. *The art of construction: Projects and principles for beginning engineers and architects.* Chicago: Chicago Review Press.

Snyder, Inez. 2005. *Sand to glass.* New York: Scholastic.

Taus-Bolstad, Stacy. 2003. *From clay to bricks.* Minneapolis: Lerner Publishing Group.

Shape Walk

Before the Walk

During the preschool years, children begin to learn cognitive concepts, such as shape, color, size, space, and number, and all the words associated with these concepts. Younger children learn by doing, and walks focusing on a particular concept offer an ideal way to help them actively learn about a concept. Of course older children are more familiar with shapes, but can still benefit from looking for and focusing on a simple concept such as shapes, not only in buildings and other structures, but in nature as well. They may even be surprised to discover the number of things composed of simple shapes, such as circles, squares, and triangles.

For many shapes—from the standard geometric ones to the more generic groups such as stars, crescents, and diamonds—they've been given the shape name of the particular form they most resemble.

Whether or not something is a true geometric shape matters much more to mathematicians than to children. The concept becomes even more complicated when you consider two-dimensional shapes (circles, squares, triangles) versus three-dimensional ones (spheres, cubes, pyramids). The

activities, ideas, and resources in this walk make reference to this broad range of considerations with more emphasis on the simpler concepts that younger children can grasp. Older children may become interested in the subtle distinctions of more complicated shapes from octagons or ovals (ellipses) to the fascinating puzzles of three- or four-sided pyramids.

This walk is not intended to emphasize right or wrong answers from the children, but to help them develop greater awareness. How children define shape will be related to which characteristics they notice most (for example, things with four corners are rectangles). Their definition offers a clue to their thinking process, which for each child is obviously right. Looking, measuring, comparing, and discussing are all ways of helping children notice more details in the learning process.

Taking shape walks encourages children to

- observe the shapes of many things
- notice and match shapes
- identify the characteristics of common shapes and learn their names

- categorize objects by noticing specific characteristics
- make some generalizations about objects that are particular shapes

For younger children, look at the pictures in Tana Hoban's shape books. These wordless books capture many shapes in sharp photographs and offer a great starting point for focusing attention on this concept. Some pages emphasize circles, some squares, and some combinations of several shapes.

After looking at the books, ask the children to look around the room and tell you what shapes they see. Ask whether they would like to go exploring for shapes around the house or building or outside. The book *Look Around: A Book about Shapes,* by Leonard Fisher, is also good for noticing basic shapes in common objects.

Words to Use and Learn

angle	curve	octagon	side
circle	diamond	oval	spiral
cone	equal	pyramid	square
corner	heart	rectangle	star
cube	oblong	round	triangle

Things to Bring on the Walk

✓ a spiral notebook that includes the children's questions and notes about experiences that might interest them (provocations), and for noting your observations of the children during the walk

✓ a camera

✓ clipboards and paper for the children

✓ writing and drawing tools

✓ measuring tools, such as tape measures, rulers, or string

✓ some shape books

✓ small paper bags with a different shape outline drawn on each bag and some counters (such as beans or poker chips)

✓ backpacks or paper bags for collecting things

 ## During the Walk

Consider using some of the following suggestions during the walk to help children learn about shapes.

Identifying Shapes
When outdoors, notice the shapes in garages, houses, windows, doors, roofs, mailboxes, traffic signs, cars, trucks, trees, bushes, patios, outdoor furniture, bird feeders, and trash cans. Many buildings, especially apartment buildings, use shapes for architectural design. Talk about the designs made by using different shapes. Older children may want to make quick sketches of all the different places they see shapes.

Be sure to take plenty of photographs of the different places you see shapes for children to look at again later.

Comparing Shapes

Encourage younger children to locate matching shapes and talk about any size differences. Triangles, for instance, come in all kinds of varieties and sizes, but if they have three points (or angles) they are all triangles. Point out that all shapes can vary in size without changing their basic characteristics. Notice size differences, such as big squares or circles and small ones.

Measure some shapes to help you decide whether something is a square or a rectangle. Measure a diamond shape to see whether its sides are all the same size. Write down the things you find out.

Counting Shapes

Invite children to keep track of how many times they see certain shapes during the walk. Younger children can put a counter in the corresponding small paper bag you brought along. Periodically, count how many counters are in each bag, but keep the counters in the bags and tabulate the results after the walk. Older children can use the clipboards, paper, and pencils to keep a running tally of how many times they see each shape. Be sure to have them tabulate their results after the walk as well.

Collecting Shapes

Younger children can collect small stones and other small items they find to use later in shape-sorting activities. Older children might want to collect items from nature in various shapes, either standard ones, such as squares and circles, or other shapes they find interesting.

 **After the Walk**

Talk about the walk with the children. You might begin by having older children add up the number of times they saw each shape. Work with younger children to add up the number of counters collected in each shape bag. The findings of both groups can be made into graphs, if desired.

Based on the children's findings, what generalizations can they make about shapes in the environment? Which shapes appear more frequently than others? Are there any shapes they

looked for but did not find? Children might suggest that rectangles are the most common shapes, roofs have a triangle shape, things that are round can roll, building materials (bricks, blocks) are usually rectangles, patio tiles are usually square, garbage cans are usually round (actually cylinders), and some shapes from nature are circles (spheres) such as acorns, and some are oval-shaped, such as leaves. Write down the children's observations on chart paper.

Older Children

Talk about the differences in the two-dimensional shapes you saw (such as traffic signs) and the three-dimensional ones (such as evergreen trees or trash cans). Give names to the three-dimensional shapes.

Show the children the photographs you took during the walk. Invite them to examine how different shapes are "hidden" in the environment. Then suggest they draw pictures of an outdoor scene with the different shapes embedded in both nature and in structures or objects made by people.

Invite children to write about their experiences hunting for shapes outdoors. Were they surprised by the number of shapes in the environment? If they took a shape walk other places, such as in a grocery store or a fire station, do they think the type and number of shapes would change? What shapes would they see more or less of?

Have children write poems about different shapes, with titles such as "I'm Seeing Circles Everywhere!" "Everyday Triangles," or "Everything Has a Shape."

There are many pictures books for young children about shapes. Invite the older children to create their own books about shapes to share with the younger children.

How many shapes are there in the room? Invite children to go on a shape search and list the different shapes they see.

Younger Children

Younger children might enjoy making shape collages. Provide small construction paper shapes and glue and let the children make collages by gluing the shapes to full-size sheets of construction paper.

Invite the children to use a variety of mediums, such as paint and clay, to represent shapes. Start a gallery of paintings and clay shapes. Encourage the addition of complex shape creations.

Do any of the children have a favorite shape? If so, ask them to tell you what their favorite shape is and why. Write down their words exactly as they say on sheets of paper. Then invite the children to draw pictures of their favorite shape to accompany their dictations.

With the children, identify different shapes around the room and put labels on them.

Have the children make shape puppets to perform songs or fingerplays. Here is a fingerplay for a rectangle:

RECTANGLE

Rectangle Puppet is my name
(hold up rectangle puppet)
My four sides are not the same
(point to sides)
Two are short and two are long
(point to each set of sides)
Now count my sides—come along
1, 2, 3, 4.
(point to each side as you count)

Explain to the children that the name of a shape comes from the number of angles or points it has, for example, a triangle has three points and a square has four. Then share the poem "Angles" with children.

ANGLES

Some shapes have angles
(point to the angles in a shape)
But others do not
(hold up a circle)
If there aren't any angles
A circle is what you've got.

Angles have points
(point to the corners of the shapes)
As you can see
And they tell what the shape
Is going to be.

Triangles have three
(hold up a triangle)
Other shapes have four
(hold up square and rectangle)
But there are some shapes
That have a lot more!
(hold up pictures or blocks that are octagons or pentagons and point to the angles)

 **Revisiting the Walk**

Take shape walks in other places, such as at a construction site or in a grocery store. Before the walk, have children predict which shape they will see the most of. Younger children can use paper bags and counters to keep track of different shapes and how often they appear. Older children can keep a running tally. When you return from the walk, total the results. Were the children's predictions correct? Which shape appeared most frequently? Were there any shapes children did not see?

Books

Burke, Jennifer S. 2000. *Rectangles*. City shapes. New York: Children's Press.

———. 2000. *Squares*. City shapes. New York: Children's Press.

Carle, Eric. 2005. *My very first book of shapes*. London: Puffin.

Dotlich, Rebecca Kai, and Maria Ferrari. 1999. *What is square?* New York: HarperFestival.

———. 2000. *What is a triangle?* New York: HarperFestival.

Fisher, Leonard. 1987. *Look around: A book about shapes*. New York: Viking Kestrel.

Gabriel, Nat, and Ronald Fritz. 2002. *Sam's sneaker squares*. Math matters. New York: Kane Press.

Hill, Eric. 1986. *Spot looks at shapes*. New York: Putnam.

Hoban, Tana. 1996. *Shapes, shapes, shapes*. New York: Mulberry Books.

———. 1998. *So many circles, so many squares*. New York: Greenwillow Books.

———. 2000. *Cubes, cones, cylinders & spheres*. New York: Greenwillow Books.

Onyefulu, Ifeoma. 2000. *A triangle for Adaora: An African book of shapes*. New York: Dutton Children's Books.

Patilla, Peter, and Liz Pichon. 2001. *Starting off with shapes*. Hauppauge, NY: Barron's.

Schlein, Miriam, and Linda Bronson. 1999. *Round and square*. Greenvale, NY: MONDO.

Schuette, Sarah L. 2003. *Rectangles*. Mankato, MN: A+ Books, An imprint of Capstone Press.

Yates, Irene, and Jill Newton. 1998. *All about shape*. New York: Benchmark Books.

Color Walk

Before the Walk

Colors are everywhere! What better time to talk with children about colors than during walks throughout the year? Each season is its own showcase of colors, giving young children endless opportunities to increase their vocabularies and observation skills. Color walks are also opportunities for older children to fine-tune their observation and descriptive-language skills. In fact, they may decide to keep a "colors journal" and write about how the colors change during different times of the year.

Exploring colors on a walk provides children with opportunities to

- observe and compare all the different shades of the same color in nature

- notice changes in the colors of things, such as leaves, foliage, or snow, over time and think about why they change

- learn what colors are used for certain signs, for example, red for stop, yellow for caution

- consider the most common colors for various things, such as houses, roofs, or cars

- think about how colors look in combination as in houses, gardens, and all around them

Before searching for colors outdoors, find out what the youngest children know about colors. Are they able to identify the basic colors of red, yellow, green, blue, purple, orange, black, brown, and white? If not, collect a variety of books about colors or invite them to make color collages using colored construction-paper scraps. Talk about the colors children are wearing each day. Make a note of colors children struggle to identify and be sure to point out examples and take photographs of those colors during the walk.

For younger children, make color-charting sheets in advance so they can keep track of how many times certain colors appear during the walk. To make the charting sheets, use crayons to make large, different-colored dots down the left side of plain sheets of white paper. When the children see a color that is on their sheet, they make a mark next to it.

Challenge older children to think about which colors they might see most often as well as least often during the walk. Have them keep track of the colors during the walk and compare the results to their predictions. Do the children have favorite colors? Have them keep a tally of the number of times they see their favorite colors during the walk.

If there are children in your group who speak a language other than English, invite them to share the words they use for different colors or color-related concepts.

Words to Use and Learn

blend	complexion	mix	shade
bright	dye	multicolored	solid
color-blind	gradation	opaque	spectrum
colorful	hue	primary colors	tint
color wheel	iridescent	secondary colors	tone

Things to Bring on the Walk

✓ a spiral notebook that includes the children's questions and notes about experiences that might interest them (provocations), and for noting your observations of the children during the walk

✓ a camera

✓ clipboards and paper for the children

✓ writing and drawing tools

✓ sunglasses

✓ a tape recorder or other recording device

✓ backpacks or paper bags for collecting things

✓ paint color samples from a paint store

✓ color-charting sheets for younger children

 ## During the Walk

Consider using some of the following suggestions during the walk to help children learn about colors. If your group includes younger children who do not know all of the colors yet, be sure to point out examples. When you teach the name of a color, it may help children remember it more easily if you connect it to something in the environment. For example, you might say, "This color is orange; orange is the color of these leaves," or "This soil is brown; brown soil, brown dirt."

Encourage older children to notice how many different shades there are of certain colors, for example, the different shades of blue or green. Upon closer examination, are some things not the color children thought they were? If children notice an "in-between color," how would they describe it? Is it mostly green or mostly brown? Does it contain more than two colors or more than three colors?

What Makes Color?

Do the children know why things are certain colors? If you pick up a leaf in the sunlight and then carry it to the shade, does its color remain the same? When you put on a pair of sunglasses, does it change the color of things? What might that tell the children about how colors are made? Help children understand the concept of how color is created by encouraging them to notice that light plays a big role in determining the color of things. If children have questions about colors that you cannot answer, write them down and help the children research the answers later.

Finding the Paint Store Colors

Use paint color samples from a paint store to help identify colors by holding the samples next to things, such as leaves, flowers, buildings, or cars. Is there a color in the environment that isn't identified on the paint samples? If so, which colors are closest to it? What would children call the new color? Why?

Seasonal Colors

Certain colors dominate certain seasons of the year. Identify the season when you are taking your walk and have children look around for the colors that appear most often. If you are walking during the summer, which colors do you see the most of? What about in the fall, winter, or spring? Ask the children to speculate why certain colors appear more frequently during certain seasons.

Moody Colors

Colors evoke certain feelings or emotions. Ask the children how certain colors make them feel. Do the colors remind them of anything? Write down what the children say about colors and moods or emotions; these comments may be helpful later on when children are thinking about ways to document their learning about colors.

Counting Colors

Invite younger children to list how many times certain colors appear using the color-charting sheets you prepared in advance. One way to organize this activity is by assigning certain colors to certain children, for example, one child could be on the lookout for green, another for brown, and so on. When a child points out a color, have the children stop and look at the color to reinforce color recognition. Or take color-specific walks. During one walk, look only for the color yellow. During another walk, look only for the color blue. Keep track of the number of times the color appears and share that information with the children after you return from the walk.

Counting Car Colors

Find an area to sit where the children can safely observe passing cars. Depending on the ages of the children, spend between five and ten minutes keeping track of the colors of cars you see.

After the Walk

Back inside, help the children tally the results of any color searches or counting activities they may have done during the walk. Which color did they see the most examples of? Which did they see the fewest examples of? Are the children surprised by the results? Why or why not? What other general observations can children make about colors?

Older Children

One project older children may enjoy is an ongoing color mural, which requires that children take a walk looking for colors during each season of the year. Cut a sheet of white paper the approximate length of a wall. Divide the sheet into three or four equal-size sections or panels to represent the seasons of the year. Whenever the children walk during a different season, have them add to the mural by painting the same general scene and how its colors change according to the season. Children can also add photographs taken during the different seasons. Display the mural throughout the year.

Invite the children to write a story about a world without color. What would a black-and-white world look like? Would the children like to live in a world without color? Why or why not? Challenge older children to consider how the world might be different if all people were the same color, such as all white or all black. How might that affect the way people around the world treat one another?

It's not easy being . . . ? Find a recording of Kermit the Frog from *Sesame Street* singing the song "It's Not Easy Being Green." Have the children listen carefully to the lyrics as you play the song. Afterward, ask the children to recall a few of the words or lines. Then, invite the children to make up their own lyrics to the song using a different color such as purple or red. When they are finished writing them, have the children share their songs with the rest of the group.

Have the children write haiku poems about different colors. Haiku poems consist of three lines that do not rhyme: the first line contains five syllables, the second line contains seven syllables, and the third line contains five syllables. Make sure children understand that syllables are the breaks in a word. For example, *red* has one syllable; *yellow* has two syllables; *magenta* has three syllables; and *aquamarine* has four syllables. Read some examples of haiku poetry to the children if needed. Here is an example of a haiku about blue and green.

BLUE AND GREEN

Shades of blue and green
Ocean colors carry me
Home across the waves.

Invite the children to describe their favorite colors using their senses. Write the following sentences on chart paper. Have children fill in their favorite color and complete the sentences:

1._____ tastes like_____ .
2._____ smells like_____ .
3._____ sounds like_____ .
4._____ feels like_____ .
5._____ looks like_____ .

After the children have filled in the blanks, invite them to share their sentences with the group.

Younger Children

If the children completed color-charting sheets during the walk, make sure you work with them to tally the results and discuss them. Why do children think certain colors appeared more often than others?

Invite the children to color or paint pictures of the colorful things they saw during the walk. For example, have them choose one color from their color sheets and draw or paint pictures of all the things they remember that were that color.

Write the names of different colors on index cards. Read the colors you have written to the children. Then invite the children to help you find those colors in the room and label them.

Invite children to make their own color books. Make blank books by folding sheets of paper in half and stapling a folded construction-paper cover to the pages. Write "My Color Book" on chart paper and have children copy the title on the covers of their books. Children can dedicate one or two pages to specific colors and draw pictures of or write about things that are those colors.

Each day, place one color of paint in the easel area, plus white. Encourage the children to paint using only that color and white. As they paint, suggest they mix white with the color to make new shades of the same color. Use new vocabulary to describe their actions, such as *base color, shades, mix, blend, warm colors,* and *cool colors.*

Read books and poems and sing songs related to colors and rainbows. *Hailstones and Halibut Bones* by Mary O'Neill or *Red Is a Dragon* by Roseanne Thong are two books to start with.

 **Revisiting the Walk**

Take a color walk with the children several times during each season to see how the colors change. If there is a paint store or home improvement store nearby, call to arrange a time when an employee can demonstrate for the children how to mix paint to create new and custom colors.

Books

Cabrera, Jane. 2000. *Cat's colors*. New York: Puffin Books.

Dahl, Michael. 2005. *White: Seeing white all around us*. Mankato, MN: Capstone Press.

Ehlert, Lois. 1998. *Color zoo*. New York: Scholastic.

Fosberg, John. 1997. *Ice cream colors*. New York: Little Simon.

Gonzalez, Maya Christina. 2007. *Mis colores, mi mundo/My colors, my world*. San Francisco: Children's Book Press.

Hoban, Tana. 1995. *Colors everywhere*. New York: Greenwillow Books.

———. 1996. *Of colors and things*. New York: Mulberry Books.

Lionni, Leo. 1959. *Little blue and little yellow: A story for Pippo and Ann and other children*. New York: McDowell, Obolensky.

McKee, David, and Beatriz Pullin. 2006. *Los colores de Elmer/Elmer's colors*. Chicago: Milet Publishing.

O'Neill, Mary. 1989. *Hailstones and halibut bones*. New York: Doubleday.

Parker, Victoria. 2004. *White with other colors*. Chicago: Raintree.

Rodrigue, George, and Bruce Goldstone. 2001. *Why is blue dog blue? A tale of colors*. New York: Stewart, Tabori & Chang.

Schuette, Sarah L. 2003. *Yellow*. Mankato, MN: A+ Books.

Thong, Roseanne, and Grace Lin. 2001. *Red is a dragon: A book of colors*. San Francisco: Chronicle Books.

Winne, Joanne. 2000. *White in my world*. New York: Children's Press.

Big and Small Walk

Before the Walk

Listen to a young child speak, and at some point you are apt to hear her describe herself as "bigger than her sister" or "taller than her friend." Providing children with hands-on opportunities to experience classification and measurement concepts is one way to help them develop a positive attitude toward and an understanding of basic mathematical concepts. Calling attention to the size of things and asking questions helps reinforce mathematical vocabulary and clarify potential misconceptions. The intent of the walk, however, is not to emphasize right or wrong answers, but to enable children to begin to develop greater awareness and understanding of the concept of size. How children talk about size will be related to which characteristics they notice most and what objects they are using for comparison.

Find out what young children already know about size concepts before the walk. While they play in the block area, ask open-ended questions about the size of the various blocks, such as "I need a block that is bigger than this one, Jordan. Please find a bigger one for me." Reading picture books that focus on size concepts is also an excellent way to begin discussions about size.

Older children who are already comfortable with basic measurement concepts can be challenged to think about more sophisticated ways of measuring very large objects that involve addition and multiplication.

Walks that focus on concepts of size provide children opportunities to

- **consider the size of things**
- **notice, compare, and match sizes**
- **categorize things by noticing specific characteristics**
- **make generalizations about objects that are certain sizes**
- **clarify terms and increase vocabulary**

Words to Use and Learn

big	great	length	small
compare	high	little	tall
diameter	huge	massive	tiny
enormous	immense	minuscule	tremendous
grand	large	petite	wide

Things to Bring on the Walk

✓ a spiral notebook that includes the children's questions and notes about experiences that might interest them (provocations), and for noting your observations of the children during the walk

✓ a camera

✓ clipboards and paper for the children

✓ writing and drawing tools

✓ standard measurement tools, such as measuring tape and rulers, and nonstandard measuring tools, such as yarn and string

✓ backpacks or paper bags for collecting things

✓ counters, such as beans or poker chips

During the Walk

Consider using some of the following suggestions during the walk to help children learn about size.

Observing Size

Look for things children can hold in their hands or hold with another child. Ask them questions about the items as you walk along. For example, you might ask, "Is the rock you're holding bigger or smaller than this rock on the ground?' "Is the rock you're holding in your hand bigger or smaller than Ian's rock?" Or point to things that children will not be able to hold, but that they can still use to make comparisons, such as "Which car is smaller? The red one or the green one?" Reinforce vocabulary by restating children's words and sentences, for example, "Yes, Ian's rock is smaller. Your rock is bigger than Ian's rock." After children are able to compare the sizes of two objects successfully, encourage them to compare three objects, and so on.

Measuring Size

Use the measuring tools—both standard and nonstandard—you brought and encourage the children to use the tools to measure different objects. You could begin by choosing two objects that are close in width or height. Invite the children to guess which is bigger or longer. Show the children how to use the string as a nonstandard measuring tool by working with another child to mark where the string stops on the object and where to hold it to continue measuring. After they have finished measuring, have another child record how many string lengths equaled the size of the object. Then have children measure the

other object. Which one was bigger? Were their predictions correct?

Challenge older children to think about "bigger" and "smaller" in more sophisticated ways. For example, if a tree is taller than a house, does it mean the tree is bigger than the house? If the house is wider than the tree, does it mean that the house is bigger than the tree? Why or why not? These are opportunities to introduce other measurement words and concepts, such as height, width, and diameter.

How Many Things Are Bigger, Smaller, or the Same?

Invite children to keep track of how many things are bigger than or smaller than a chosen object. Begin by giving one child an object to hold, such as a pinecone. Then give another child a small paper bag and give a few counters to other children. Children can take turns spotting objects during the walk and asking, for example, "Is that plastic bucket bigger than the pinecone?" If the object spotted is bigger, a child puts a counter in the paper bag. After a few minutes, help the children count the number of counters in the bag and ask them how many objects were bigger. You can follow the same procedure for objects that are smaller and objects that are the same size.

The Biggest and the Smallest

While walking, keep a list of which things the children see are the biggest and the smallest. As children discover an object that is bigger or smaller than the object identified as the biggest or smallest so far, cross out the old object and add the name of the new object to the list. This activity gives children opportunities to use superlatives, such as *biggest* and *smallest*. Restate their observations to encourage new vocabulary, for example, "We said that the tree by the house was the biggest tree so far, but now we see a tree that is bigger. This tree is bigger than the one by the house." Right before you go back inside, circle the biggest object seen and the smallest object seen. Discuss the list when everyone is inside.

Measuring Things That Grow

Another idea might be to measure things that grow or change, such as flowers or fast-growing plants. During one walk, measure the height of a flower. During another walk a week or so later, measure the plant again. Is it bigger? Has it grown? Is it now bigger than other things that are next to it?

What Shall We Measure This Time?

Prior to taking other walks to look for big and small things, determine beforehand what category or group of things the children will look for. Will they look for cars that are big and small? Will they look for buildings that are big and small? What ideas do they have of things to look for?

 **After the Walk**

Back inside, help the children tally the results of the size search or any counting activities they may have done during the walk. What were the smallest things they saw? What were the biggest things they saw? Are the children surprised by the results? Why or why not? What other general observations can the children make about size?

Older Children

For older children who took actual measurements of things, what did they discover? What was the largest thing they measured? What was the smallest? Which measuring tools were the easiest to use? Which were the most fun to use? Why? Invite the children to think of other standard and nonstandard measuring tools they could use during the next walk.

Consider talking with older children about "scale," that is, one object's size in relation to that of another object. Invite them to create small clay models of different things that are to scale. This encourages children to think about proportion or size relative to other things. For example, if they first molded a dog from clay, how might they represent a person's actual size in relation to the dog's size? Is the person three times as large as the dog? Four times as large? What is a dog's size in relation to a car? How might children determine an object's size in relation to something else?

Invite the children to write stories or poems about themselves when they were "little" and now that they are "bigger." Write the following sentences on chart paper for the children to complete to get them thinking about the ways they have changed:

• When I was little, I used to think that . . . [children complete the sentence and expand on it]

• Now that I am bigger, I think that . . . [children complete the sentence and expand on it]

Explain synonyms to the children. Tell them that synonyms are words that have the same or nearly the same meaning, such as *small* and *tiny*. Many size-related words are synonyms. Invite the children to work with a partner or in a small group to think of synonyms for words that have to do with size, such as *large*, *small*, *tall*, and *thin*. Consider creating a thesaurus for the children to fill in as they discover new synonyms.

Have the children ever heard the phrase "Bigger is better"? What does it mean? When might someone say "Bigger is better"? Is bigger always better? When is bigger not better? Have children write what they think about the phrase "Bigger is better" and whether they believe it to be true or not.

Invite the children to create paper-bag puppets with names such as Bernie Big, Misty Miniature, and Shelly Small. Then invite them to create a puppet show involving those characters. How did the characters get their names? What happens to them in the puppet show? Encourage the children to put on the puppet show for younger children.

Younger Children
Talk about what the children observed about size during the walk. Discuss their findings, such as the biggest thing they saw and the smallest thing they saw. Can they make any generalizations about size in the environment? Were there several objects that were the same size?

Look around the room. What things are big? What things are small? What things are in between? Work with the children to create labels that identify objects as big, little, or medium in size. Did children see things from the walk that were about the same size as objects in the room? For example, might a pinecone be about the same size as a toy car or a Duplo piece?

Read books that focus on other concepts of size, such as *Biggest, Strongest, Fastest* by Steve Jenkins.

Have children make "Big, Bigger, Biggest" posters and "Small, Smaller, Smallest" posters. For example, on the "Big" posters they could draw a variety of objects of different sizes—a big shoe, a bigger shoe, and a biggest shoe.

Create a special word wall dedicated to size, including drawings or magazine pictures of things that demonstrate size, such as a tall building or a small insect.

Organize the blocks in the block area by size and label the containers by size of block.

Revisiting the Walk

How have the children's ideas about size changed since the last walk? Have they learned new concepts related to size that they could look for during a new walk, such as height or width? If you took measurements of things that grow, check on their progress. Write down the measurements and compare them to your last measurements when you return from the walk.

Books

Challoner, Jack. 1997. *Big and small.* Austin, TX: Raintree Steck-Vaughn.

Coffelt, Nancy. 2009. *Big, bigger, biggest!* New York: Henry Holt.

Gordon, Sharon. 2004. *Big small.* New York: Benchmark Books.

Granowsky, Alvin, and Mary Lonsdale. 2001. *Big and small.* Brookfield, CT: Copper Beech Books.

Gunzi, Christiane. 2006. *My very first look at sizes.* Minnetonka, MN: Two-Can Publishing.

Harris, Nicholas. 2004. *How big?* Detroit: Blackbirch Press.

Hillman, Ben. 2007. *How big is it? A big book all about BIGness.* New York: Scholastic Reference.

Hoban, Tana. 1997. *Is it larger? Is it smaller?* New York: William Morrow.

Jenkins, Steve. 1995. *Biggest, strongest, fastest.* New York: Ticknor & Fields Books for Young Readers.

———. 2004. *Actual size.* Boston: Houghton Mifflin.

Lewis, J. Patrick, and Bob Barner. 2007. *Big is big (and little, little): A book of contrasts.* New York: Holiday House.

Miller, Margaret. 1998. *Big and little.* New York: Greenwillow Books.

Patricelli, Leslie. 2003. *Big little.* Board books. Cambridge, MA: Candlewick Press.

Ribke, Simone T. 2004. *A garden full of sizes.* New York: Children's Press.

Ring, Susan, and Gloria Ramos. 2006. *Big or small?* Bloomington, MN: Red Brick Learning.

Light and Shadows Walk

Before the Walk

On summer days children and their families or providers often look for shady spots to sit—and it's not often we stop to explain to children what makes the shade. In some languages, the word *shadow* describes shade, but the English language uses different words, so many children do not automatically make the connection between shadow and shade. In addition, light from the sky can dramatically alter the color of things and how they are perceived, depending on the time of day. Taking a walk to observe shadows and light offers an ideal opportunity to help children learn the concept of shade and pay closer attention to how light affects so many things in the environment.

A light and shadows walk also provides opportunities to

- learn what causes shadows and how they change

- observe our own shadows and how we can make them do things

- play games using shadows

- consider how sun and shadows relate to telling time

- notice colors and how colors are affected by light

- discuss how light affects the overall feeling of a place

Before the walk, find out what children know about shadows and light. Read Robert Louis Stevenson's poem "My Shadow" to younger children. Ask them if they know what a shadow is, and if they have noticed their own shadow. What do they think causes shadows? Why did the boy in the poem say his shadow was lazy and still in bed?

Demonstrate for younger children how shadows are produced. For example, gather a doll and a flashlight. Stand the doll on a table placed near a wall. Shine the flashlight at the doll, toward the wall, so the light comes from one side. The light should cast a shadow on the wall. Explain that because the doll is an opaque object, it blocks the light and makes the shape of the object—a shadow—on the wall.

Move the flashlight around so that it shines at different angles on the doll. Move it closer to the doll, and then farther away. Does moving the light change the shadow? If you want, measure the shadow cast from different angles and write down your findings. Plan to go outside at different times of the day to look for and measure shadows.

For older children, discuss how light and shadows are important for artists trying to capture the essence of outdoor scenes. Find examples of artistic styles, such as impressionistic paintings, which emphasize light and its changing qualities.

Talk about how civilizations thousands of years ago relied on light and shadows to tell the time. Discuss the accuracy of ancient sundials and how sundials are still used today. Invite children to create their own sundials to experiment with during and after the walk. To make a sundial, place a small piece of clay in the center of a paper plate. Push a pencil into the clay so that the pencil will stand erect with the plate at its base. Place the sundial in a sunny window. Look at it every hour during the day, and each time draw a line where the shadow of the pencil is on the plate. Think about what the finished picture looks like.

Take walks to observe shadows at different times during the day and at different times of the year. Late afternoon in the fall has a very shadowy feeling, which is different from the same time of day in the spring or summer. If you want, repeat activities on subsequent trips. After the first walk, save your notes, including descriptions, measurements, and the children's observations, so you can compare them. It might be a good idea to date everything you write down so you get results for the whole year. You and the children can write up a firsthand report of what happens to shadows, light, and color over a year's time.

Words to Use and Learn

angle	elongated	muted	shape
bright	glaring	opaque	silhouette
dark	hazy	reflection	size
diffuse	intense	shade	sundial
direct	light	shadow	sunshine

Things to Bring on the Walk

✓ a spiral notebook that includes the children's questions and notes about experiences that might interest them (provocations), and for noting your observations of the children during the walk

✓ a camera

✓ clipboards and paper for the children

✓ writing and drawing tools

✓ chalk

✓ measuring tools, such as tape measures, rulers, or string

✓ a thermometer for measuring air temperature

✓ backpacks or paper bags for collecting things

✓ a tape recorder or other recording device

 **During the Walk**

Consider using some of the following suggestions during the walk to help children learn about light and shadows. Should children discover other aspects of light and shadows that interest them, be sure to help them pursue and later document those interests.

Observing Light and Shadows
On a sunny day, look for shadows as you walk. Notice the shadows of cars, trees, houses, street signs, people, animals, and anything else you can find.

Plan to look for shadows in the morning and again in the afternoon to see whether they look different.

Let the children observe their own and each other's shadows. Can they make their shadows move or do things? Observe what happens. Change the shape of the shadows by moving arms and legs or by sitting down.

Look for shadows from clouds, airplanes, kites, balloons, and clothes hanging on lines. If you see some shaded areas in the yard or street, try to figure out what is producing that shade.

Are the shadows the same on both sides of the street? Are there places where there aren't any shadows?

Do moving things also have shadows? Do you see shadows from moving cars, running animals, or other things? What do you notice about the shadows as they move?

Ask the children to describe the light. Is it bright or glaring? Is it gray and hazy?

How does the light affect colors? How do shadows affect colors? What color are shadows? When light is absent, what happens to colors? If light affects colors, might the same objects appear to be different colors at different times of the day? Why or why not?

Invite the children to use paper and crayons to try to match colors of certain objects or things. Show younger children how colors can be blended to create new colors. Be sure to save the children's drawings so they can compare them to other drawings they make of the same objects at different times of the day, noticing how more or less light changes the color of things.

Take photographs of shadows and the children's shadows at different times of the day.

Experimenting with Light and Shadows

Plan to go outside several times during a day, beginning in the morning. Trace around the children's shadows in the morning. Mark where their feet were placed so they can stand in the same spot again later in the day to see what happens to their shadows. Each time you go outdoors, measure their shadows or have older children help each other measure their shadows. When are their shadows the longest? When are they the shortest? Test frequently throughout the day to see how their shadows change. Write down the length after each measurement. Are their shadows in the same places each time, or do they move? Make lines to show where their shadows are each time.

Take along a thermometer to measure the air temperature in the sun and in the shade. Talk about the difference and note why it feels cooler in the shade.

Measure the size of shadows from parked cars, signs, fire hydrants, trees, and other objects. Measure either with the ruler or tape measure or by pacing. Keep track of the size of those shadows. Measure them at other times of the day to see if they also change.

Take photographs and try to get the shadows in the pictures.

Go out on a cloudy, hazy day to see whether you can find any shadows.

Playing Games with Light and Shadows

Play games with the shadows, such as running and standing in someone else's shadow, connecting shadows with rope or chalk, tracing around shadows, and catching shadows in hoops.

Play shadow tag, designating the large shadows of buildings or trees as safe zones. Play "Don't Step On My Shadow" tag. The child who is "it" tries to step on the shadow of another child who then becomes "it." For the most fun, play this game in a large open area.

 **After the Walk**

Discuss the children's observations of shadows and light. Make a list on chart paper of their observations. Can the children make some generalizations about light and shadows based on their observations? An example might be that shadows are longest late in the afternoon, shortest in the middle of the day, and there are no shadows when it is cloudy. Ask younger children how these observations compare to the doll's shadow you made inside before the walk. Think about how the size of the shadow may be related to the position of the light in relation to the object.

Older Children

Were any older children interested in the color changes they observed during different times of the day? Did they use crayons to try to capture the colors of a particular scene each time they went outside? If so, they might refer to their sketches to help them make larger sketches or paintings.

Invite the children to research ways to create sundials. Display them in a Sundial Gallery.

Invite the children to write "shadow skits," short, silent plays performed behind a white sheet with a projector. Have the performers stand between the

light and the sheet. Can other children guess what the shadow skits are about?

Encourage the children to write imaginary stories about shadows and light with titles such as "The Day My Shadow Walked Away," or "A World Without Colors."

How does light (or the lack of it) affect people's moods? Is there a connection between too little exposure to light and one's overall mood? Have the children keep a journal over two weeks' time describing each day's weather and how they felt that day. After the two weeks, the have the children read their entries. Did they notice any connections between the day's weather and their overall feelings during the day? What generalizations can the children make about light and one's state of mind?

Show the children some of the photographs taken during the walk. Have each child choose a photograph and write about it in some way, for example, in a short descriptive piece or in a poem. Or challenge children to write about a photograph without using the word "shadow." Invite children to share their writing with others after they are finished.

Younger Children

Younger children might enjoy creating a "shadow mural" on a large sheet of paper. Have the children draw pictures of trees, houses, cars, and other objects on the paper, leaving room between the items. Then have the children make shadows of the things they drew on the mural. Encourage the children to consider where the light comes from and whether the shadows will all go in the same direction.

Show the children multiple photographs of the same thing taken during different times of the day. Ask them whether the things look the same or different. If different, how are they different? Are the shadows the same or different? Are the colors the same or different?

Read the story *What Makes a Shadow?* by Clyde Robert Bulla, and try out some of the suggested experiments. Have the children try to make shadows at night at home; the next day, they can tell the group what they noticed. It might be a good idea to let families know you have suggested this activity so they can help find a good light source and a wall or counter surface. Ask the children to notice shadows in their houses at night. Are there shadows of furniture, plants, railings, doors, and other objects? Perhaps the children can make pictures of the things that made shadows in their houses. Ask adult family members to write down their child's observations to help them remember.

Create a class story on chart paper called "The Day My Shadow Walked Away." Invite each child to contribute lines to the story. When the story is finished, read it back to the children. Then invite the children to create illustrations for the story. Display the class story and the children's drawings in the room for others to enjoy.

Add new words related to light and shadows to an existing word wall.

Sing songs, read poems and stories, or have children perform fingerplays related to shadows and light.

 # Revisiting the Walk

Shadows and light change dramatically, depending on the time of day and season of the year. Take multiple walks with the children throughout the year to observe and document the changes. During each walk, measure shadows, write down or record observations, or draw pictures that demonstrate how colors change too.

Books

Anno, Mitsumasa. 1988. *In shadowland*. New York: Orchard Books.

Berge, Claire, Derrick Alderman, and Denise Shea. 2005. *Whose shadow is this? A look at animal shapes—round, long, and pointy*. Minneapolis: Picture Window Books.

Bulla, Clyde Robert, and June Otani. 1994. *What makes a shadow?* New York: HarperCollins.

Dorros, Arthur. 1990. *Me and my shadow*. New York: Scholastic.

Gibbons, Gail. 1983. *Sun up, sun down*. San Diego: Voyager Books.

Hoban, Tana. 1990. *Shadows and reflections*. New York: Greenwillow Books.

Paul, Ann Whitford, and Mark Graham. 1992. *Shadows are about*. New York: Scholastic.

Riley, Peter D. 2002. *Light and dark*. Milwaukee, WI: G. Stevens.

Ring, Susan. 2003. *Light and shadow*. Mankato, MN: Yellow Umbrella Books.

Royston, Angela. 2002. *Light and dark*. Chicago: Heinemann Library.

Sayre, April Pulley, and Harvey Stevenson. 2002. *Shadows*. New York: Henry Holt.

Stevenson, Robert Louis, and Ted Rand. 1990. *My shadow*. New York: Putnam.

Swinburne, Stephen R. 1999. *Guess whose shadow?* Honesdale, PA: Boyds Mill Press.

Tompert, Ann, and Lynn Munsinger. 1984. *Nothing sticks like a shadow*. Boston: Houghton Mifflin.

Waters, Jennifer. 2002. *Bright lights and shadowy shapes*. Spyglass books. Minneapolis: Compass Point Books.

Appendixes

General Permission Slip

Dear Families,

An important part of our regular program includes walks in the neighborhood and a few field trips into the community. These are an excellent means of expanding children's knowledge of the world around them. Children are always well supervised on excursions. Please sign and return this permission slip for our records.

Sincerely,

_____ has my permission to go on neighborhood walks and

community field trips while attending _____ program.

_____   _____
Date   Parent/Guardian Signature

Notification and Permission Slip

Dear Families,

We are planning a walk to _____ on _____.

We will be leaving at _____ and returning at _____.

What we hope to see and learn:

Special notes:

Sincerely yours,

· ✂

Please sign and return the field trip permission slip below.

_____ has my permission to participate in the walk to

_____ on _____ .

_____   _____

Date   Parent/Guardian Signature

Hey Kids! Out the Door, Let's Explore! by Rhoda Redleaf, copyright © 2010.
Redleaf Press grants permission to photocopy this page for classroom use.

Walk Planning Form

Type of walk:
Purpose of the walk:
Words associated with the walk:
Activity or question introducing the walk:
Things to watch for or collect on the walk:
Anticipated problems during the walk:
Follow-up activities after the walk:
Will we revisit the walk? When: Purpose: Activity:

Walk Checklist for Staff

Walk destination: _____

Phone number: _____

Date: _____

Time: _____

Schedule: _____

_____

_____

❏ Extra help secured

    Name and phone number: _____

    Name and phone number: _____

    Name and phone number: _____

    Name and phone number: _____

Snack for trip: _____

Special needs: _____

_____

❏ Family notices complete

❏ Site arrangements complete

❏ Name tags organized

❏ Planning forms complete; copies made for all adults on walk

❏ First-aid kits ready

❏ Permission slips returned

Hey Kids! Out the Door, Let's Explore! by Rhoda Redleaf, copyright © 2010.
Redleaf Press grants permission to photocopy this page for classroom use.

Orientation List for Volunteers

1. Thank you for helping make this exciting experience possible.

2. Familiarize yourself with the information sheet for this walk. It gives you the purpose of the walk, the logistics of the walk, points of interest to talk about, and special words to explain to the children.

3. You will supervise the children on your list. You might play a little game with the children to help you learn their names. Try to relate personally to each child, making sure each one feels comfortable.

4. Some children may feel unsure in new situations. Comfort them, hold their hands, and smile. Talk about how fun it is to go away for a little while and then return and tell others about it.

5. During the course of the walk, talk with your group of children about what they are seeing. Frequently repeat the names of things, and also repeat or retell information that may be given by the leader. Encourage questions and stimulate curiosity with your own questions. For example, "I wonder how that works?" or "Why do you think she is doing that?"

6. Anticipate situations such as puddles, mud, or obstacles in the path. Prepare children so possible difficulties may be avoided. Tell the children what to do, such as "Take a big, big step over the puddle," instead of saying "Don't step in the puddle."

7. Children must be with adults at all times! They should not be left alone or sent alone to find another group or teacher. Getting lost is a frightening experience and should be avoided. Go to the bathroom as a group, if necessary, or find another adult to supervise the children who are waiting.

8. Stay calm and relaxed. Your calmness will reassure children in any situation. Remember, most problems can be solved with a few moments of calm thinking. Play little games such as "I Spy Something Red" or "What Do I See?" in situations where children have to wait and are growing restless.

9. Have fun. Enjoy what you're doing and share your enthusiasm—then the children will share your enjoyment.